UNFAIR!

Kimberly Griffith & Dr. Terry Gunnells

EMMA JAY PUBLISHING

MONTGOMERY, AL

Published by Emma Jay Publishing
6237 Wares Ferry Road
Montgomery, AL 36117

Book design by Lawrence Gunnells

Library of Congress Catalog Card Number
97-71192

ISBN 0-9657347-0-6

Printed in the United States of America
March 1997
FIRST EDITION

Dedicated to:

This book is dedicated to the memory of
Eric and Amy Smith.
They died much too young.
May this book sustain their memory
for many years to come.

Table of Contents

Introduction

I am honored to have had a part in initiating and writing this book. In deference to any contribution that I might have made to it, I do not want anything to distract from the story it contains, nor the therapeutic value intended by it. Everything in it, including the tenor and flow, is Kim's story and she alone had firsthand knowledge of what she saw on July 17, 1995. Only she can tell us how she felt when she first stumbled on to the scene that awaited her when she came home that afternoon. Her family dynamics and what transpired previous to the tragedy are a part of her history, and no one knows it better than she does. She has had to walk the lonesome valley of grief alone, for none of us belonged there with her. We can only journey with her through the pages of this book and learn what she will allow us to know and feel.

May I emphasize that I am only the wordsmith; it is Kim's story. The business part of this book falls to Kim's responsibility since my Code of Ethics does not allow me to have a dual relationship with a client. I am her therapist and this book must continue to be a part of the therapeutic relationship. I am sworn never to exploit a client.

Few people have experienced such destructive forces and yet remained determined to make good of life. When Kim was six, her mother attempted to smother her twice, and when she was ten, her mother committed suicide. At the age of fifteen, Kim's father was charged, and later exonerated, for a fatal accidental shooting. Her marriage of eighteen years was less than fulfilling, and her daughter, Amy, had a learning disability. Finally, at the age of thirty-nine, she experienced the homicide of her children and suicide of her husband.

At times it might seem that she is writing to her children, Amy and Eric, her husband, David (Dave), or even to God. This, too, is a part of her therapy. She wants this story to help others who have experienced the loss of children or survived suicide, and she also hopes that it will be beneficial to caregivers who can learn from her experience. Kim hopes that the telling of her story might give her more insight into what has happened to her, give her life meaning, and somehow, bring about resolution.

Around the first of May 1996, I suggested that as a part of

her therapy Kim write some of her feelings in a journal. Later I suggested that she write a book. At first she was really enthusiastic about it, but then she began to have doubts that there was enough information to do anything of that magnitude. When I saw her obvious concern, I said, "Keep a tape recorder with you, and every time you think about what's happened to you, just switch it on and start talking. Say whatever you feel and don't worry about how others will react. Just tell the recorder your innermost feelings and I will transcribe it. Take some time to think about it, edit it and be sure it says what you want it to say." She bought a mini-cassette recorder and began to tell her story. I combined what she recorded with some of the information she had discussed in therapy sessions and edited it for print.

Some directions the book has taken have been due to the gentle pressure I applied to insure the healing Kim needed. We owe her a debt of gratitude for sharing her personal story with us.

When Kim came in for her first therapy session, she looked at me with sad eyes and said, "My husband shot my children and then shot himself. I'm a widow and childless mother. Do you think that's fair?" After what she said seemed to her like several minutes, being stunned, I said, *The most unfair thing I have ever heard.* From the perspective of my answer, I have decided to help Kim tell her heartrending story — a story that was even difficult for me to comprehend as being real. The words *unfair, unfair* continue to echo in my head.

There are many things about the death of Kim's husband and children that she will be unable to explain. I suggested that she let facts and feelings flow naturally from her troubled mind.

Kim and I are writing this book for several reasons. First, we hoped it would give her some relief from the mental anguish of her grief work. Second, she wanted to explain some of the dynamics of suicide and grief in conjunction with her unanticipated and fiercely unwanted tragedy. Third, I wanted her to tell her story as a healing instrument by which I hope she will find closure on her soul-wrenching nightmare. Fourth, Kim wanted this book to be a memorial to Amy and Eric, her two lovely children whose pictures appear on the front cover. She also hopes to use this medium to eclipse any suspicion that might surround their deaths by telling what she knows about it with as much detail as she possibly can.

Kim sincerely hopes that her story will help others who are caught in the trappings of grief, and especially where suicide or homicide of children is involved.

The untimely deaths of Kim's family do not follow the normal life cycle. However, any loss, whether large or small, creates grief that is the natural way the psyche deals with disappointment and change. Perhaps some of Kim's expertise in grief, learned from her personal experiences, will be helpful to others who have reason to grieve.

In order for you to get the full benefit of this book, I ask you to imagine coming home from a routine day at work and finding your thirteen year old daughter dead on the kitchen floor, your husband sitting on the top step of the stairs, dead with blood all over him, and your fifteen year old son dead on the floor of his bedroom as Kim did on July 17, 1995.

If anything like this ever happens to you, you will be thankful for shock that allows reality to seep out in installments. When Kim experienced shock, even the law enforcement agents were confused about how unaffected she seemed to be by the horrible scene, and, at what I refer to as her "flat affect"— no facial expressions. She was so impervious to the seriousness of the moment that the authorities initially suspected that she had something to do with the murders of her family, which was "as far as the East is from the West" from being true. Kim had absolutely nothing to do with the events of that infamous day.

As a part of Kim's therapy, she developed a "Life Script" that began with her "birth myth." This is how the story surrounding her birth came down to her through others, as to how she was received by her family. As well as she can ascertain Kim was a wanted child. As her mother became more emotionally unstable, that changed, and Kim became, in her mother's mind, a part of her problem. We will develop some further thoughts about this in the chapter on Family Dynamics where we will write about the suicide of her mother that occurred when Kim was ten years old.

This is a book about dysfunctional families, prescription drug abuse, learning disabilities, marital discord, suicide and grief.

1

A Day That Shall Live In Infamy

The main part to Kim's story centers around the day her world fell apart — July 17, 1995. Every time I think of that sad day in July, I think of the words of President Franklin D. Roosevelt when he responded to the bombing of Pearl Harbor, "This day shall live in infamy." I have decided to make this the title of this chapter, "A Day That Shall Live in Infamy."

Kim was feeling a little tired that day from the traveling the family had done on vacation and dreaded to go back to work even though she enjoyed her job. When something as catastrophic as this happens you would think it would be on a day when there were warnings, but it was just a normal work day.

She and her family had driven home from vacation on Saturday and gone to church on Sunday as they almost always did. The whole family was tired but still seemed to be excited about the few days of fun and sun they had enjoyed. The weather had been perfect. David had rented rooms in a neat condo right on the beach and things seemed to have gone really well. One day Kim was romping on the beach and a few days later, she was rolling in sorrow.

When they first moved to Virginia, things had not gone well at all, but now things were much better. Kim and her family had bought a nice townhouse in a middle-class neighborhood. The house was white, two stories, with vinyl-type siding on it. The front entrance had a little stoop over it and the whole atmosphere said "Welcome". They had begun to establish themselves in the community of single dwelling houses and townhouses. The children were growing into young adults.

Eric was fifteen and overcoming some of his adolescent problems. He was making new friends, including a couple of girlfriends, doing a lot of art work, and was going to begin guitar lessons the next week. Eric was looking forward to being sixteen and getting his own car. Kim felt that her wonderful son was a charming young man.

Amy was thirteen and had never been happier. She was using her winning personality to overcome her learning disability. Going on church tours, talking to people about the Lord, and getting to know the kids from the church were Amy's life.

Her face always had a smile on it. It is ironic that she died with a smile on her face.

David had been more irritated than usual. The things he did, in retrospect, seemed more serious. At the time Kim just thought, "Well, that's just Dave." He did not come to bed at all that night. His unusual behavior just got lost in the shuffle of a new work day. Kim thought it would all pass over as usual.

Because of the nature of the events that took place on July 17, 1995, I have asked Kim to tell her story from this point on. I would hope that the readers would journey with her through that fateful day.

Kim Tells Her Story

When the alarm went off I got up as usual. David got dressed and went to work as he usually did. I just tried to stay clear of him to give him some time to get over whatever it was that was bothering him. The way he was acting was not appropriate after the family had just had such quality time together. However, I felt that he needed a little space. I just don't remember much about our interchanges that morning. There was nothing that caused me to suspect that he was going to do what he did.

The children were out of school for the summer so they were sleeping in. After I got ready for work, I told them I was going to buy some groceries for lunch. They just grinned and barely acknowledged my presence. I got some of their favorite things, like pizzas and snacks, so they would have some "goodies" to eat that day. Then I went back by the house, put everything away, went upstairs, went in each one's room, hugged and kissed them, and told them good-bye and that I would see them that afternoon. Then I went to work as I did on any other work day. How was I to know that that would be the last time I would ever kiss them or see them alive? I am so glad the last thing I did with my children was to kiss them and tell them I loved them.

I drove the thirty minutes to work and took some time to get organized after having been out for a whole week. Lab activities were kinda slow at work that morning. During my break time, Dave called me. We had what seemed like, at the time, a normal conversation. In retrospect, I think something in his voice was different. He kept insisting, "Is there anything you want me to do for you?" I kept saying, "No. No, I've done everything I needed to do." I said, "No. No problem. I don't have anything going on." He said, "I have a doctor's appointment at twelve today." I said, "Okay, that's fine. Just let me know how it turns out." I just kept on doing my work. Sometimes I wonder if his call was not an effort to lure me somewhere so he could kill me, too. Of course, there's no way to know. My therapist helps me to realize that to dwell on what didn't happen takes away from the energy I need to deal with what did happen.

The kids usually slept until about lunch time so about one o'clock, at the end of my lunch break, I decided to check on them. I called and there was no answer, and I thought, "They're really tired. I'll wait about fifteen minutes and try to call again." I let the phone ring until I got the answering machine and I thought maybe they were just outside piddling around. I tried to put it out of my mind.

I had to help a fellow worker in another building across the street from my office, and when I finished, I went back to my regular work area. It was about two o'clock and I kept thinking, "I need to check on the kids." I called again and there was still no answer. Our rules were that when they were home alone they were never to leave the house without letting me know where they were going. Amy and Eric were good kids and didn't ever violate that rule. I got concerned and called Dave's office to see if he would go by the house and check on them. When I called, the people at his office said that he had left some time before lunch and they hadn't seen him since so they didn't know where he was.

This timetable probably eliminates Dave's having killed the children earlier than lunch time. No one knows for sure but the police investigation report indicates that David left work at approximately 11:15 A.M. A neighbor told the police that she saw his car in the driveway at 12:00 P.M. Someone also reported seeing David leave the house and return later which caused the authorities to speculate that he probably wanted to kill me, too, but just couldn't figure out how to get me in the picture.

I thought, "It's two o'clock and he's had plenty of time to have gone to his doctor's appointment and be back," so I tried to beep him. Then I started to get just a little more worried and I thought about taking off work, but since I had just been on

17

vacation and didn't need to lose any time, I convinced myself that I was just being paranoid. Maybe they were all outside, David took them out to lunch, or something like that. I tried to rationalize everything and I thought, "Well, there's probably no problem," and about that time, I started getting really busy at work which took my mind off of it for a while. I thought, "Well, everything will resolve itself. I'm sure everything is okay." Still, I kept calling and leaving messages on the machine, "Please call me back. If you are there, please let me know." I didn't ever get a call back. I guess the messages were still on the machine when the police checked it.

At about five o'clock I had this uneasy feeling. I was unusually nervous and upset. I just got in my car and began driving toward home and the long drive gave me time to calm down. When I came up the street where we lived, I saw David's car in the driveway. I thought, "Well, good, he's home and everything's fine because he would have called me by now if things were not all right, so I'm sure everything's okay."

My neighbor was outside digging in her yard planting some flowers and I stopped and talked to her for a few minutes. I asked her what was going on with her these days. We chit-chatted and I went on to the house, tried to open the front door and it was locked. That seemed unusual because Dave almost always got home before I did, started supper, and had the front door unlocked. Most afternoons he grilled something on the patio. There were usually a lot of things going on around our house but it was a little bit too quiet and the front door was locked. I just had this uneasy feeling that something was wrong. I opened the door and called out and no one answered back. Like I said, everything was deathly quiet. Then I walked to the kitchen and saw my little Amy lying in the middle of the floor. When I ran over to her I could tell from the first glance that she was dead. She was so still. Her eyes were closed and she had a peaceful look on her face. Her face was pale, blue-colored, and kind of grayish blue around her mouth. She was on her back with both arms thrown behind her head.

I stumbled toward the front door in a daze and then I looked up at the top of the stairs and saw Dave, sitting up but slouched over with blood all over him. Shock set in at that point because I didn't scream. I didn't cry or do anything. Immediately I went to the door and called my neighbor who was still working in her yard. By now I was screaming and I said, "Help me! Help me! She's dead! She's dead! They're dead!" She came over and started screaming, "Kim, where's Eric? Where's Eric?" The house was too quiet and I knew he was dead, too.

I didn't know where he was and the obvious place to look was in his room. As I walked up the stairs, which was the longest walk I've ever walked, I held the stair rail. As strange as it sounds, I began to hear the words of a song that we had sung in church just the day before, almost like a chorus. The song was, "I love you, written in red." Why these words flooded my mind, I'll never know but that's the only thing that held me up. I walked up the stairs and saw that David had been shot. He had the gun in one hand and extra bullets in the other yet it didn't dawn on me what had really happened. When I went in Eric's room and saw him lying on the floor, I realized that he had been shot, too. He was face down and covered in blood. His black and white comforter was all wrapped around him, like maybe, he was trying to protect himself with it. I don't know but that's the way it looked. I now wonder if David had not put the comforter over him and tucked him in as if he were asleep.

My memory is so faded. It's hard to even remember what it was like. I do remember that Eric had a baseball bat beside his leg as if he had picked it up to try to defend himself. One of his little socks was halfway off his foot, like maybe he was just beginning to put it on or something. I don't know. He was already partially dressed because he had on his shorts, a tee shirt and his billfold was in his pocket.

I saw that they were dead and I just wondered who had killed them, even though I saw the gun in David's hand. At that point my neighbor was saying, "Kim, they're dead. They're all dead. We've got to call 911." I said, "Okay," so I called 911 and told the operator, "My family's dead. I've come home from work and they are all dead. They've been killed." The 911 operator said, "Ma'am, stay right there. We're on the way." They were there right away.

When the police came, I walked out of the door. I still had on my white laboratory uniform pants and my hands were in my pockets. Since I wasn't crying or screaming or anything, I'm sure it appeared that I was very calm because I was stunned. For a while I went in and out of shock.

They immediately treated me as if I were a suspect because one officer said, "Hold it right there, ma'am. Stop! Don't move an inch! Take your hands out of your pockets. Let's see your hands." So I held out my hands so they could see them and the officer said, "You stand right over here. Don't you move." A couple of people stayed with me and the others went in to look. They were upset at what they saw. One officer said, "What happened here?" I told them that I came home from work and this is what I found. I had to tell them the whole story about when I last saw them. They asked a lot of other questions, most of which I cannot remember.

When they were sure that I was not going to run away or anything, they said, "She's in shock. Let's just take her across the street." I went across the street to my neighbor's house and eventually ended up in bed in one of her bedrooms.

Everybody Had A Right To Know

I remained relatively calm until I heard that the TV News cameras were at my house and I went ballistic! I was hysterical! It was like, "How can you do this to me? I refuse to let them take pictures of my children!" One of the female attendants said, "Ma'am, there's nothing we can do. It's public domain if it's outside your house. They can't take any pictures inside but they can take pictures on the outside."

I had a horrible feeling that as the bodies of my children were being wheeled out, they were going to be on television for everybody to see. Sure enough, the story was on the radio, television and in the newspapers. My friends at work heard about it on the radio first and then saw my babies' pictures on television. The blood-splattered window of my son's room was published in the paper the next day. Naturally I kept thinking, "No privacy. No dignity. Public knowledge. They said everybody had a right to know."

Outpouring Of Love

Through this chaos, however, I received the most tremendous outpouring of love I have ever experienced. My friends, neighbors, and even total strangers grieved with me, supported me, sent cards, offered money, or rushed to my side to meet every need and I felt so much consolation. There were people all over the country praying for me. I don't know everyone who helped but to those of you who showed me such love, you know who you are and I want you to know that I am eternally grateful. May God reward you in this life and the life to come. I had never known such compassion.

I Didn't Hold My Children

I wish that I had held my children in my arms but I didn't even get to touch them one last time, except at the funeral home which didn't really count. Now I just wish I had picked them up, rocked them, held them and told them how much I loved them. The hugs and kisses that I gave them before I went to work that morning didn't count either. I needed one more hug and kiss and I probably always will.

My Last Visit To The House

When I went back to the house to pack up everything, I decided to lie down in the very spot where each child had died. I lay down in each spot and cried and wondered how they died. I first lay down on the kitchen floor where I found Amy and wondered if she looked up and saw the same ceiling at which I was looking, or did she look directly into heaven? Trying to reenact what happened, I wondered what she was thinking — if she thought anything — if she blacked out, or called for me to help her? Sometimes I can hear her calling for me now. Did Jesus come and meet her halfway, or what was it like for her? Was she totally taken by surprise, or was she afraid? Did Dave catch her off guard, or was she aware that he was going to kill her? Is this why she was running away as the autopsy seems to indicate? I don't know what happened and I wish I did so I would not have to speculate for the rest of my life.

Then I went upstairs in Eric's bedroom and lay down in exactly the same spot where he died. I was face down like he was and I wondered what happened to my baby. What happened to him? What was he thinking? Was he trying to defend himself, or was he trying to defend Amy? Did he realize it was his daddy killing him? What went on in that house? Who put his favorite comforter on him?

How Did David Do It?

David used an old vintage, pearl-handled 38 caliber pistol that had been given to him by his aunt who also served as his grandmother. She reared David's mother and lived with his parents until she died at the age of 95. David shot each child three times and himself once.

For some time I felt that David had caught Amy totally by surprise while she was standing in the kitchen, possibly getting something out of the refrigerator, and killed her instantly with no pain or fear involved. It was somewhat comforting to think that she wasn't aware of what happened or who did it. After reading the autopsy report with my therapist, it now seems that she was running from David and that she was on a lower level than he was when the first shot was fired since the entry of the bullet was on a downward trajectory. David apparently was on the stairs above her. The second shot was fired into her back at close range and then the third was probably from the front as she was lying on the floor. Of course, I am convinced that he was trying to make it as painless and quick as possible. Each shot seemed to be strategically placed to insure that death came quickly.

Initially I believed that he had killed Amy first and then went into Eric's room, who by now had heard the commotion and was putting on his clothes to see what was happening. This concept would have allowed him to get the baseball bat to be used as a weapon against an intruder. However, it now looks like David shot Eric first. How did Eric get the comforter? Was he sitting on the bed and just gathered it up when he saw what was about to happen to defend himself? Apparently when he saw what was going on, he raised his left leg, drawing his knee toward his body to protect himself. One bullet grazed his left thigh.

Knowing Eric, he could have just had the baseball bat lying there beside his bed, so it might be a coincidence that it was where it was.

The evidence seems to be that Dave shot Eric from the front and then twice in the back to make sure that he died instantly. I'm really not sure how to explain the splattered blood on the window but I'm told that where there has been a close range shooting, there's always tiny particles of flesh, blood, and possibly bone fragments all around the crime scene. However, now I've come to believe that he shot Eric first, Amy heard the commotion and was running away from David when she was shot.

David then left the house for a short period, drove away in his car and returned, at which time he shot himself. I wonder if he went to the children to make sure that they were dead, or if he shot them the last time after he returned to be sure they were not suffering. Was this when he covered Eric with the comforter as if he were asleep, or could it be that he had not even shot them when he left the house, changed his mind about going to the doctor, and returned to commit the homicide/suicide? Could he and Eric have had one of their ongoing childish arguments and David left and became so angry that he returned to do what he did? No one knows. Then, of course, if he had been planning this for a long time, the spontaneous theory would not work.

The comforter continues to be a puzzle to me. Since there were no bullet holes in it, it is almost certain that it was placed on Eric after he was shot. I had not seen the comforter since that day until I saw it at my father's house spread out on a bed, and I ran to it and smelled it because I remembered how the house smelled when I first discovered the bodies of my family. It did not have the smell of death on it so I am assuming one of the neighbors washed it along with several other things that came from the house. One day I plan to ask the police or someone about the comforter so I can have some things settled in my mind.

As I tried to question the police about some things that were unclear in my mind, they became reluctant to answer my questions. I checked off the items that I wanted returned. The ones I did not want, such as the gun and pill bottles, I assume were destroyed. I wish now I had kept them but at the time I could not stand to see them. They were instruments of destruction that had killed my family.

| 2 |

Family Dynamics

Kim said that she thought she knew how much one's family of origin plays in his or her life, but she has been forced to re-examine David's and hers. In all that has happened she has learned that their families failed to prepare them to deal with life's pains and pleasures in a normal way. She feels that what they experienced in their families of origin determined their emotional stability and gave them faulty patterns by which to solve problems. The way Kim grieved the loss of her mother was indicative of her lack of emotional stability. She has come to realize that as an adult it is her responsibility to change whatever patterns she learned that are unhealthy.

This chapter will deal with Kim's and David's family dynamics as she saw them. She will reiterate some things David told her about his family, how her family influenced her, and the way hers and David's family developed over the eighteen years that they were married.

Kim wants to apologize to anyone who might be portrayed in this book in a less than favorable light. If telling this story were not a vital part of her total grief recovery therapy, she probably would not have disclosed some of the things in this book, but it is, and she hopes it will help everyone in both families to grow from it.

Kim continued to say that she could not help but wonder what was so wrong with her family that her mama had to commit suicide. All she ever wanted out of life was a family of her own. When she got it, she built her whole world around it, and the one person she expected to help her keep it in tact destroyed it with his own hands. She must live with the unanswered question as to where her own family went wrong.

Dave's Family Of Origin

Dave (David) was Kim's husband of eighteen years who killed their two children, Amy and Eric, and then killed himself. He was so passive that he very seldom spoke to Kim about his family in a negative way. As any son should, he loved them but he felt that they played a major role in his unhealthy emotional development.

28

Since Kim did not grow up in David's family, she can only relate to them through what she learned from being married to their son; therefore, her perception was revealed as accurately as she could express it.

Dave's childhood, according to what he told Kim, was spent not knowing the emotional tenor of his parents. He felt like he identified with his depressed mother, and that this was part of why he was depressed most of his life. This caused him to harbor so much resentment because he felt as if he had learned unhealthy, depressive attitudes from his parents, and that his emotional damage was beyond repair. David believed his nervous system was affected and that the depressed lifestyle could possibly cause harmful effects such as failure in life. Kim never dreamed it could cause him to be so miserable inside and to develop personality disorders that were so out of control.

David's mother and father were in their late twenties when they were married. Since his mother was reared by her aunt she felt obligated to live with her and take care of her. So, David's mother and father lived with his mother's aunt whom David looked upon as a grandmother.

David's brother was born first and was viewed by him as being "the apple of his parents' eyes." He always believed that he could not live up to the standards of his older brother. David was aware that he was not planned and felt like he was an accident. He later came to the conclusion that he had a learning disability much like his daughter, Amy. School was a struggle for him. When he was twelve or thirteen he had a viral infection or something that affected his kidneys and had to stay out of school for a year. This threw him further behind in his education.

When David went to college he studied criminal justice with ambition to be in law enforcement. Of course this never panned out. He became an insurance adjuster which was investigative to some extent.

During David's early life his family struggled financially. By the time he and Kim were married, his dad had advanced to the management level. The family was financially sound when David died.

David had some resentment toward his mother because she would not deal with his father's alcohol problem. He felt that his father's preoccupation with alcohol had deprived him of the father figure that he needed to develop into manhood. This probably accounts for his inability to deal with Eric's growth into manhood and the volatile arguments between the two of them.

Kim had some resentment toward them for not spending any time with her children. Her feelings have nothing to do with how David came to understand his role in his own family. His actions years before demonstrated what he learned from his mother and dad. They were not mean to David and always provided the material things that he needed. At least they deserve some credit for holding their family together. David perceived them as being preoccupied with other things and not having much time for him as a child. His dad spent most of his time working or drinking. Dave said that his dad tried to be discreet with his drinking by keeping his vodka in the trunk of the car, but almost everyone knew it was there. This type of lifestyle took up most of the family time and left little quality time for the children. His mother was not involved with alcohol but spent a great deal of energy trying to cope with it. Of course, this left the children deprived of the emotional support they needed during their formative years of development, or as in most families where alcohol is involved, created some guilt and shame.

David's maternal great aunt, whom he referred to as grandmother, lived with his family and his recollection of this was that she was a domineering woman who was always arguing with his dad. His only brother seems to have his life in order and is apparently successful. He was very helpful to Kim during the tragic losses of David, Eric and Amy, both during the funeral preparation and by allowing her to live in his home for a few weeks.

Kim's Family Of Origin

Kim was born when her mother was twenty-five and her dad was thirty-two years old. Her mother was reared in a shanty-type house and experienced near poverty living conditions. Kim's grandmother was in her forties when her mother was born. Her mother's daddy was in his twenties and an alcoholic.

When talking about her mother, Kim says that what happened to her children made her wonder about her own birth and how her mother really felt when she was pregnant. When Kim was pregnant with Eric, her oldest child, she said that she had never been more excited. She had a husband that she loved and whom she thought really loved her, and she had more energy than she normally had. The euphoria of approaching childbirth was indescribable. Kim wishes that she could know that her mother felt that way about her. She wondered if she was excited. Did she dream of having a little girl that would fulfill her every need as Kim did when her Amy was born? Exactly what did she feel? Considering what transpired when she was a child, Kim has doubts that her mother was excited. Her mother was emotionally absent. She lived in a world of uncertainty and felt incarcerated in her mother's emotional prison. Kim feels that she has forgiven her mother because she does not want to be a victim the rest of her life. Through her therapy several years before I met Kim, she learned that it would serve no purpose to ruminate about the hurt, the void, and the losses caused by her mother's emotional absence. This probably could have been more damaging than her mother's physical abandonment when she committed suicide.

Until recently Kim was not aware of how her relationship with her mother created some basic fears in her. Because her mom was so emotionally unpredictable, she never felt a consistent flow of love.

Kim was a perfectionist and always wanted things done right. She carried a lot of guilt about her mother's death, which she did not realize until it came out in therapy several years ago. The therapist that she saw then did a lot of Rational Emotive Therapy and some inner child work. He tried to help her go back and grieve for her mother, but she said that she never really knew what grief was until she began grieving for her children when they were killed.

Kim can remember her dad telling her that it was all right for her to cry at her mother's funeral but she could not grieve. Years later, while she was sweeping the kitchen floor, a light came on in her head, and she realized that she was not responsible for her mother's death. Up to then she had thought that if she had only been a perfect child, her mother would not have killed herself. Kim always felt that if she had just been a better kid or done more or done better — more, more, more — things would have turned out better and she would still have her mother.

Finally through a lot of hard work in therapy, she came to realize it did not matter what she did, she could not change the past. She could turn cartwheels, have the most immaculate house, the best paying job, or be the smartest student in her class but it did not matter because all of those things wouldn't bring her mother back. Anything she might have accomplished would not change the past, and that's what she now sees she was trying to do. I often remind her that this is her compensatory behavior, always over compensating for her guilt or feelings of inadequacy. This new revelation was a real awakening for her and she began to put away a lot of perfectionistic tendencies that she had had for most of her life. She did not have to impress anyone or be a people pleaser, and it was a real refreshing time for her emotionally. Counseling helped her grow stronger, but it still did not change David who seemed to grow more and more miserable.

During her previous therapy, Kim read some really good books, one of which was *Telling Yourself the Truth*, which taught her how to combat the lies that she was telling herself about herself. It taught her how to be her own friend and she got some meaningful growth out of the contents of that book which she highly recommends.

I have tried to help her identify her fear of allowing her emotions to have free course in her life. She has been able to see that the feelings of abandonment are based on real life experiences because she has been abandoned by every significant person in her life. She is so angry! I made her promise not to abandon herself but to love herself and take care of herself.

This fear of abandonment, up until now, has blocked Kim's ability to establish and maintain the kind of intimacy that she has needed. It probably made her more needy than the average person and yearn to be loved and appreciated, yet she did not want to admit it. She has had a history of fitting wherever and with whomever she found herself. She developed a "rag doll" personality — wherever someone put her she just tried to make the best out of it — and, of course, all of this stems from her childhood. Chances are she chose David, knowing that he was not able to sustain a meaningful emotional relationship with her. Whether she knew that or not, it became evident that she did a good job of choosing someone who was just as damaged or worse than she was. This always seems to be the case unless wounded children get help to recover.

Being emotionally intimate takes a lot of hard, exhausting work. Kim has learned that intimacy is impossible without trust. She says that she is so bitter at times realizing that her relationship with her mother retarded her inner child emotionally so much that she has little or no foundation of trust, and all of this made her a perfectionist. It made her work so hard to serve the needs of David and play both sides of their relationship because she was afraid David would not do his part. She has learned through therapy, that when one tries to carry the full load of the relationship, the end result is anger and resentment on both sides. This sets up a typical love/hate relationship that is the pits for both partners. She says that she is so ticked off, and wonders why she had to have such a role to play in a tragedy written by someone else, probably her mother, and in a major way, David. Then she is so thankful that she has been released from this prison. Oh how she wishes it could have happened before she lost her two precious innocent children because of her family's worsening dysfunction.

Kim was very young when the mother she never had became so afraid of living that she sought relief from her pain in a bottle of poison. Because she was too young to understand, she put so much blame on herself. At that age she knew of no other recourse but to see herself as the cause of everything that took place in her world.

Kim remembers two occasions when she was about six that her mother tried to smother her while she was sleeping. Her mom put her hand over Kim's nose and mouth and kept it there until she writhed and struggled for air. Then, suddenly her mom released her grip and gave Kim a big hug. She was afraid of herself and what she had almost done. Although Kim was very small, she said that she knew then that something just was not right, but she was not sure what it was. She never fully trusted her mother after that. Throughout Kim's childhood, she always wondered what she had done to make her mother want to kill her, and she remembers her mother telling her time and time again, "Don't ever get married and, especially do not have children." You can imagine how this made a little child feel. Kim felt as though she had caused her mother's pain and she felt so unwanted. It was a time of tremendous ambiguity and at times Kim said, "I felt loved, and at times, I felt hated."

Kim said she always felt that her family was a mess and she felt so messed up with it. I think it was Pogo who said something to the effect, "We saw the enemy and he was us." This sounds much like what Kim was saying about her family.

Can you see why Kim wanted to be in the medical profession so she could help fix people who were hurting, and then later, spent the money, time and effort to get a Master's degree in counseling? She wanted everyone to just give her someone to fix — send all the birds with broken pinions to her — let her feel well by helping the downtrodden, the emotionally sick folks of the whole world. She was the Statue of Liberty, you know. I suppose she felt that if she could fix enough people, somehow she could vicariously be healed.

Until now it sounds as if Kim was not just a controller, she had both ends of the gamut. She was not going to be controlled by anyone. As a child she dreamed of turning sixteen and being able to drive so she could get a car and drive herself to school and church and not be dependent on anyone. Perhaps this is why Kim put such a high priority on getting Eric a car when he became sixteen. Of course she never got the chance to buy him a car. He was killed before his sixteenth birthday. Not only did she have an obsessive need to control but she had such a fear of being consumed by someone in a relationship. She said that she could now see that she had shut down her emotions and not allowed anyone in her inner circle but her two children, and they were taken from her in such a despicable way.

If Kim could have understood that dodging her emotional issues was so unhealthy, and could have met them head-on before now, things might have been different in some ways but I doubt it would have changed David's behavior. I have tried to convince her that responsibility never looks back — it can only be in the present and future. It is not her responsibility to resurrect her dead mother, nor Amy, Eric, and David, but to rise from the dead world of sorrow and live again. If she does not do that, her children will have died in vain. In their honor and memory, she must live again and help others live who are trapped in childhood traumas and dysfunctional homes, not in a driven, out-of-control way, but in a very deliberate, calculated, healthy way. She might even be able, if it is indeed feasible, to set up a grief institute for parents who have lost children or for victims of suicide. I have tried to convince her that if she dreams the right dreams, they will come true. I told her that my father always told me, "You get what you want if you know what to want."

I asked Kim to pray this prayer: "Please God, help me to

draw as much good from this tragedy as is possible. If you will help me Lord, I will squeeze every ounce of good out of my life for your sake and the sake of my children. I want to be a true 'wounded healer' who has been healed myself so I can show my helpees my scars and they will know I understand their pain."

Kim knows the pain of abandonment. It has caused a lifelong trail of tears. But it is time for her to stop the tears of hurt and cry some tears of joy — joy of seeing others benefit from her past pain and loss, to win some victories over negative forces, such as the ones that have tried to destroy her.

I had Kim to repeat, "I forgive you, Mama! I'm trying to forgive you, David! I forgive you, little Kim! And most of all, I forgive you, big Kim! You must feel free to grow unencumbered by the baggage from the past. Feel free to start over, chart a new course, seek a path of genuine comfort — you are now the master of your own destiny. Plan your life and live your plan."

As I listen to the words about Kim's family, I realize that she lived in a patriarchal world. There was not a significant woman in her life. The house was her dad's and everything revolved around him because there was no mother there. Even when her mother was alive, Kim recalls that her dad was not good to her mom. On at least one occasion, Kim's dad blacked her mother's eye. She never did things that would upset her dad because he was the only rock on which she could stand, otherwise she would have drowned in the sea of uncertainty in which fate had put her. Kim feels her daddy deserves credit because she did not have to live in poverty. She had health care and she was given an education. She was not hooked on drugs nor was her plight so bad that she chose to be an unwed mother to have someone to love her. In spite of all she had, she was unhappy and never felt really appreciated by her father, and then later by her husband. The ability to receive love should have been learned from her mother who was unable to teach her healthy emotions. Kim felt as if her dad was always absorbed in his work and did not allow her and her sister to have fun or act happy. Kim's sister, who is younger than her, has had a lifetime of depression and unhealthy emotions. She came to live with David and Kim one time, and when Kim set her up in her own apartment, her sister felt hurt and abandoned about which Kim says she feels so badly.

I asked Kim if she had been a boy, would her dad have blessed her like Isaac did Jacob, or would she have been Esau and missed her blessing? Has she ever really had her father's blessing? She said that while she was at home, she was her "daddy's little girl," but he was not pleased when she insisted on going away to college.

Kim remembers when she was a little girl, after her mother had committed suicide, that her daddy, who was a steel worker, had a back injury that required surgery. She and her sister had to live with their father's sister for almost two months. During this time her aunt complained aloud about how expensive it was to keep extra children and what a burden it was. Kim felt unwanted and unworthy by what was being said by her aunt. The lack of being affirmed by a father often causes girls to seek the blessings of men throughout their lives. Of course this does not mean that they will necessarily become promiscuous but there is just a little something missing, and in Kim's case, she needed the approval of a male.

Of course, Kim said that she would never know what scars her daddy bore from his childhood or from her mother's illness and suicide. She knows that her dad was reared by a mother and three sisters. His dad died when he was 8 years old.

The Structure Of Kim's Family

The structure of Kim's family, which consisted of David, Eric, Amy and her, had evolved into a matriarchal one. Looking back on the almost eighteen years David and Kim had been married, she could see this evolution taking place. It happened partly because David's emotional quotient was never at a mature level and partly because she was already accustomed to being protective of herself, and naturally this would include her need to protect David, or anyone in her nest just like any other mother hen. Perhaps if she made a mistake, it was to include her children in her inner circle rather than allowing them to take their rightful position on the periphery. However, even an honest mistake like that, if it was one, could not have caused a distortion of the magnitude that would have caused David to do such a sick, despicable thing. I have asked Kim to repeat, "I am not responsible — David, you are!"

Kim Trusted David

Among all her family members, her mom, dad, and

in-laws, she trusted David the most. The one person she expected to help her keep her world in tact destroyed it with his own two hands. She will never understand how, or why, David could have done such a thing. What in the world could have made him so angry or sick that he would have killed his children? It made no sense for David to destroy their family. Everything about their deaths seemed so *unfair*.

Kim Loved David

Even though Kim resents David for not loving her and the children the way she wanted him to, she believed in him with all her heart. She is mad because she loved him when she thought no one else did and she stood by him when no one else would have. She said that she babied, nurtured, and encouraged him, but she did not get anything in return. Throughout their marriage, Kim wanted to love someone and she wanted it to be David, but he would not let her. He made her laugh and she enjoyed being with him because he was easygoing and did not get all bent out of shape like her dad always did. David was a lot of fun when they were first married, but that all changed. Now she resents him for the unfair way he treated her by killing her children.

David Resented the Children

The one thing that really bothered Kim was that she always felt as if David resented the children. If she bought them anything he resented it, or when she wanted him to be involved in anything they were doing, he resented it. He had resented them their whole lives and she is angry about that. I have not forced her to change because I know she will in due time.

He Should Be Punished

Although Kim still loves David, at times she feels as if she wants him to go straight to torment and burn forever. When she thinks about forever, she thinks that maybe not forever, but just for a couple of weeks. Then, she feels sorry for him and she says, "Well, maybe just for a couple of days or fifteen minutes." This sounds funny to those of us who read this but it is a serious matter to Kim.

If David is in heaven, like Kim understood the minister to say at the funeral, that means he is being rewarded for what he did wrong, and that's *unfair*.

She believes David should have to pay for what he has done. You might ask, "Is she not being selfish to want David held responsible for what he did?" The answer is, "Yes!" Those were her children. They came from her womb. Her breasts sustained them. Her hands cared for them. They drew emotional nurture from her heart. They were hers. They belonged to her. They should have been protected by their home, the law, society, and a higher law than humankind can make or break, but they were not They were ripped away from her and she is angry, and I allow her to be as angry as she needs to be. Like a purse snatcher, David snatched her children and ran. The only difference is, the value of her children was — well, they were priceless — they were the standard for all things worthy — they were not for sale.

Kim said that she always thought the most valuable thing in the world was satisfaction. They were her satisfaction — now they are gone and it's *unfair.*

Was Kim's Family Traditional?

When my wife, two grandchildren and I were traveling to Texas this summer, I saw a family come into McDonald's. There was the husband, wife and two children: a boy and a girl. Their grandfather was with them. He was getting old, very slow and unsteady, but so kind and considerate of everyone. The eyes of his family hardly left him. It was obvious they revered him. He was kind and loving to them and they reciprocated. I asked myself, "Is this what the term, 'traditional family', really means? Why couldn't Kim have been blessed with a family like that? Where was the love and respect in her family? Why didn't David love her and her children like that? Why didn't they totally trust one another and enjoy being together like the family at McDonald's? " When I related this to Kim, she said, "As far as I can tell, our family didn't fit any model; it was dysfunctional." Then I realized, even with a wife, husband, and two children, which should have stacked up to be so traditional, Kim's family ended up dysfunctional, and finally in a state of dissolution — not by divorce — but hers ended up with her children being killed at the hands of their own biological father. How can there be any fairness in such an end? All is well that ends well but her family didn't end well.

Who determines when a family is traditional? I suppose

the meaning of the word "traditional" changes with each culture anyway. Were the early "settlers" of America the standard? Did the fact that they were "productive" because every member of the family was expected to produce something with their own hands make them the standard? Were the "Puritans" the standard in that they would marry a stranger and grow into a loving family? Where did Kim's family fit? It was neither productive nor Puritan. The television was their baby sitter and the door of their house, like a castle gate, was supposed to protect their children. The door and all the locks could not protect them from their own father. Is that fair when children are not safe in their own home with their own father? Is that really a safe haven, a vestibule of heaven? You be the judge. I suppose you can see as the writer of Kim's story I am totally involved in it and I hope you are too.

Kim's Family At A Crossroads

Every family, sooner or later, has crises. Some are just a part of the human predicament or the life cycle, and others are caused by one or more members of the family. Usually when a family has a problem one of several things will happen. It will: (1) solve itself and soon be forgotten; (2) linger and be tolerated by the family members; (3) be resolved by counseling; or, (4) end in divorce. As Yogi Berra said, "When you come to a crossroads, take it." I guess David came to a crossroads, didn't know what to do because in his depressed state none of the options seemed to fit the problem. This confusion resulted in the homicide of his children and his suicide.

If David did this to eliminate a problem or to make life easy for Kim, it did not work. She feels like she would have been willing to have done whatever was necessary to solve the problem but David took all options from her. He did not give her a chance and that is why she feels angry. She knew she and David had a problem. Only God could have known more than her. She felt at the appropriate time that she and David would handle it together — in one of the several ways that I have already mentioned. She had even thought about divorce several times and gone to counseling alone. David had gone to counseling on several occasions and for all intents and purposes, she thought they were choosing option number two — just trying to ride it out by making the adjustments that were necessary.

How does the way Kim's family turned out relate to hers and David's families of origin? Both of them came from dysfunctional families. Neither one of them learned by experience how to handle stressful problems. Kim says that they had learned bits and pieces from church and books but they did not have a good pattern. She said, "Our families of origin were not what we wanted them to be, yet it seems that ours turned out worse than theirs." The pattern is broken now as far as Kim's family is concerned. It is so *unfair.*

Where Did Kim's Family Go?

Kim wanted to have lots of kids, more than the two that she had. She wanted a whole house full — a big family. Her dreams were to have a place where she could sink her roots down deep and raise her children up right, to give them everything she never had as a child, to give them all the love she never had. She wanted to be the mother she never had, to treat her children right, hug and kiss them, buy them things, educate them in Christian schools, teach them about God, make them feel secure and loved and that's what she thought she was doing. That's what makes it so hard for her to understand. She is the only one left and feels so cheated. It's so *unfair*. "Where did they go? They've disappeared."

I hope the readers can see the effects of Kim's tragic childhood on the way she yearned to develop a healthy family. Her experience, if we can harness it, will be of such great value in helping survivors of dysfunctional families. Kim is so unique. She is humble as "apple pie" but has the "brass" to confront and accept the truth about matters that she knows from experience will hurt people. Her advice, even though she has made and will continue to make mistakes, is more valid than that which comes from someone who hasn't "been there — done that".

3

Kim's Life With David

Kim met David in college on January 21, 1976 through a mutual friend on a blind date. At first she liked him okay. She didn't think he was anything special and she kind of thought he was a little silly. Most of her life Kim had taken everything very seriously. David was always joking and cutting up which sometimes she thought was a little childish but she grew to enjoy it.

She kept dating him and it seemed like things kinda clicked. He was fun and she was attracted to his sense of humor. Since Kim was shy and insecure, especially around men, this new relationship became comfortable for her. David was always the life of the party. He was a fraternity guy and he and Kim hung out at the "frat" house. She says that they had a whirlwind romance and she's not so sure she was ever as much in love with him as she was his lifestyle and carefree personality. When they first started talking about marriage, Kim felt like she loved him, but not as much as she should have. She talked herself into thinking, "Well, he's a good person; he's a Christian and he loves me," so she decided to marry him and they became engaged.

They were engaged for about a year. It was a long distance engagement because he was working a lot. They were together some at school, but sometimes their school schedules collided and prevented them from spending quality time together which was essential to building a good relationship.

They were married in their junior year. Kim had a year of internship left on her Med Tech B.S. degree and David lacked a full year of college. They got married in May. Kim said that she almost backed out about two months before the wedding. Her sister tried to convince her that David wasn't good for her and things like that. Kim thinks now that maybe she was right. On one occasion Kim went home to her daddy in tears, and he gave her some good advice. He said, "Kim, you're the only one who can say whether you can marry him or not. You're the only one that has to live with him."

As Kim revisits the past, she feels like she married David because they had gone so far sexually that she felt obligated to him. They didn't have sex. She was a virgin but their sexual petting had gone further than she thought it should have. With her rigid religious background, Kim felt like she had to marry David, but now, looking back, it seems so ridiculous to her. The awesome responsibility of living with another person for life demands the right reason to marry.

One time Kim tried to convince David that they should date other people for a while so they could be sure that they were doing the right thing. He cried and she felt sorry for him and consented to marry him even though it was for all the wrong reasons. Now Kim says she can see how insecure and possessive David was of her, even back then. This possessiveness continued throughout their marriage but always seemed to be so subtle that no one could see it.

Moved To Birmingham

Kim and David got married in spite of her reservations. The first year of their marriage they didn't see each other much because she was doing her internship. They moved to Birmingham and she worked from six in the morning until about three-thirty or four in the afternoon. David went to school in the morning and had an evening job, so they really didn't see each other except on the weekends. The first year of their marriage was fine. Kim now thinks that maybe it was better for them not to have had to spend much time together during their adjustment period.

The second year Kim got a job and things were still going well. They were having fun -- she enjoyed David. She doesn't remember many problems since they never argued. David was so passive. They never fussed or fought or anything like that which Kim now knows was not as good as it sounds. They didn't communicate that much.

Kim wanted to have a career but she also wanted to have children, a house and two cars. All the middle class things appealed to them so they set out to get them, or at least she did.

After they had been married about two years, Kim stopped taking birth control pills because she wanted to get pregnant. David had a lot of reservations and wasn't tremendously enthusiastic about having a child, another sign of his insecurity. Kim thinks that he was more scared than anything, but when Eric was born in November of 1979, it seemed like he was excited. He would get up with Eric and take care of him. Things seemed very normal at that point in their marriage. Kim says, "How I wish it could have stayed like that but it turned sour."

Moved To Montgomery

David's career was moving up. In January of 1980, the company for which he was working offered him a promotion and a chance to move to Montgomery, and so they moved.

They sold their house in Birmingham and bought one in Montgomery, and things just seemed like they were going well. Kim took a part-time job and then she got pregnant again. She wanted a girl so badly she could taste it. She had her boy and now she wanted a girl to go with him. Amy was born in 1982 and Kim was the most content person on earth. She had a job that she loved, two beautiful children, a comfortable house in Forest Hills (a middle-class housing development in Montgomery) that she liked. David was fine and things seemed like they were really running smoothly for their family.

Their marriage started going downhill when Amy was about a year old. Kim felt like David became competitive with the children, another sign of insecurity and possessiveness. She felt like he, in some ways, was jealous of them. He admitted to her later on, after they were much older, that he had felt jealous of them. David resented the time that Kim spent with them, and that she spent money on them. He resented the fact that Kim loved, cared for, and nurtured them so much. She said, "I never intentionally left him out and I tried to do stuff for him, too." It was not easy to constantly juggle the children and David who often had to be treated like a child.

About this time in their marriage, David became less and less there for Kim emotionally, and she was taking on more and more responsibility. When Amy was a year old, things started crumbling. David insisted that Kim go to work full time. She was working part-time every other Friday through Monday evenings. David forced her into taking a full-time job so he would not have to baby-sit on the weekends. She resented that. One time she remembers going in Amy's room and picking her up and crying and telling her that she wasn't going to have much time with her anymore because she was going to have to go to work every day and put her in day care. Amy was about a year old and just a little bitty thing and Kim hated to leave her, but that's what she wound up doing which was totally against her will.

When Kim put the kids in day care, she cried. She resented the absolute "stuffing" out of it. Not only did she resent it, but she couldn't find a job in a hospital and went to work in a private office. By the time she paid taxes and day care, she made less than her part-time pay had been. She tried to explain that to David but he refused to understand it because his motive was to escape having to baby-sit the children while Kim worked.

The fact that David would not do whatever was necessary for Kim to stay home with the children made her really resent him. She didn't feel like she shouldn't work, but she felt like part-time was enough for her to work with two small children. It was extremely hard on her to take the children to day care, and she cried every day and they did, too. She didn't like it, but she did it for several years even though it eroded the infrastructure of her family.

David never had any goals. Kim would ask him, "Dave, what goals would you like to accomplish in your life?" He just never had an answer — he never knew. The only thing he wanted to do was just have fun, sink money into his hobbies and his Civil War stuff with which he had become so infatuated. It is ironic that Eric had just completed a drawing of a Civil War officer for his dad a short time before David killed him. David didn't seem to have any ambition about his work and that would drive Kim nuts being the perfectionist that she was.

During this stressful time, Kim developed a very close

friendship with a man who was going through some problems with his marriage, and they talked a lot about it. This special friendship reminded her of what was missing in her marriage. She couldn't understand why someone was able to give her in a friendship what she needed the most from David and was not getting. This man would build her up, make her feel wonderful, and they understood one another. They mutually agreed not to do anything to hurt their marriages so their relationship just continued on a friendship level.

When Kim realized how emotionally dependent she had become on a man who was not her husband, she decided to go to counseling for the first time to seek help for herself as an individual and for her marriage. Counseling gave her a little help but not a whole lot because the whole family system needed to be fixed and they were not working together as a family.

Moved Back To Birmingham

David decided to change jobs and they moved back to Birmingham and started the cycle all over. Things were difficult financially, and Kim had to start work immediately. The children were able to go to a Christian school and Kim was happy about that. They bought a house that Kim dearly loved and got into a church with a lot of really neat people. They stayed there about two years which were the hardest years for David up to this point in their lives. It was extremely stressful for their marriage for a lot of reasons, one being that David had a female boss who was very demanding. She didn't have a car so she made him feel like it was his responsibility to take her back and forth to work. She would even call sometimes late at night and say, "I'm still at work and I don't have a ride home; come get me". He would have to drop whatever he was doing and go get her. He was really stressed out on this job.

She was putting some kind of pressure on him, but Kim doesn't know if there was sexual harassment. She asked him if they were having an affair and he said they weren't, but Kim always wondered if there was sexual temptation, or if he felt manipulated by her. There wasn't any jealousy on Kim's part which she can now see was unhealthy. It was an extremely difficult two years for David, and he decided to move back to Montgomery which was just another stressor for Kim.

About this time, still feeling very unfulfilled, Kim developed a friendship with another man. They began talking about the Bible, God, and other religious matters. They saw each other a lot and talked on the phone at other times. Kim says that she tried in so many words to let David know that she had emotional needs that weren't being met but he was unresponsive. This man gave her emotionally what she needed from David. She needed someone to give her some "attaboys" and tell her that she was smart, funny and all those things, and gradually, Kim felt like they were beginning to fall in love. She and her friend talked about it and decided not to be unfaithful to their spouses. At this point Kim started asking God, "Why? Why did you say that we had to stay married to one person for life, even if the relationship was strangling me emotionally? Why? Why? Why?"

Kim Went To Counseling

David's and Kim's marriage continued to have problems because they were not emotionally connected and she went into clinical depression. Kim says she felt like she was on a spinning wheel, always running, never getting anywhere. The more depressed she became, the more she felt like working. At one time she had three jobs, two small children, and a husband. She says that she thought that if she would just work more, try harder, do more church activities, things would get better. They didn't and she found herself slipping into despair. She was so determined, however, *not* to wind up like her mother that she sought counseling. At that time she did not believe in taking anti-depressants so she wanted to get to the root of her problem to see if that would help. Kim says she remembers praying and telling God that she felt like there was a large thorn sticking in her heart the size of a stake, and she prayed, "Please, God, remove it." It was after that prayer she learned the name of a wonderful Christian counselor in the city where she was living at that time. That therapy would later totally change her life but it didn't prevent what eventually happened to her on July 17, 1995.

Moved Back To Montgomery

The time came for Kim's family to move back to Montgomery. This was another difficult move because she did not want to leave what she had worked hard to build in Birmingham. She gave some thought as to whether she would move with Dave this time. Of course, she decided to go with him. Kim felt like

55

she needed to try one more time. She believed that the only Christian thing to do was to follow her husband. She told herself, "You're suppose to try, try, and try until you can't try anymore," so that's what she did.

A part of Kim's anger toward God now, or at least the times that she is angry with Him, is that she feels, "Well, God, I did everything like you told me to. I stuck with this man when I wasn't getting anything in return and this is the thanks I get." When Kim would talk to David, she would say, "And, oh yes, thank you, Dave, for being such a turkey. I stuck with you all of this time and you just spit in my face." Obviously, she's very angry about all of that.

When Kim's family moved back to Montgomery for the second time, she started working a part-time night shift job at a hospital, and working a full-time job in a private office. David and Kim bought a house and began the same routine they had all been used to by now.

At that point in their marriage, and probably life in general, Kim felt like she was just hanging on. She continued to talk to her friend from another city. He was like a breath of fresh air and wrote her a lot of letters of encouragement.

Kim kept trying to hold it together. She says, "I guess we did the best we could with all of the baggage we both had." It seemed like every time Kim put down roots, made friends, and had begun to accomplish some things for herself, it was time for Dave to move on again, and that's pretty much what happened until the end.

Kim Went Back To School

While the family was in Montgomery, due to the feeling of being so unfulfilled and seeking to compensate for it, Kim decided to go back to school. She wanted to get her Master's degree in counseling. Since she had gotten so much good out of counseling, like many others who have had a good experience in counseling, she thought this is what she wanted to do for the rest of her life. She wanted to help other people to see things clearly and so she went to Troy State and loved it. Kim graduated with high grades, and then couldn't find a job making nearly as much money as she was making as a Medical Technologist. Since she had two children that she was trying to support, she was not able to use the degree in counseling, and she just accepted the fact that it was going to be that way for a while. Now, however, since her children have been killed, Kim would like to go back to school and do work in suicide research and intervention.

Moved To Virginia

Dave decided to move to Virginia. Kim said that he had this dream and he thought that he was always going to be unfulfilled if he didn't do it, so he decided to move to Virginia.

Again, Kim almost decided to stay in Montgomery and keep the children here. She talked herself into being a Christian wife and followed her husband, sticking with him "through thick and thin." Kim, in anguish, says, "That's what I did. I stuck with him and he ended up 'sticking' it to me by killing my children and himself."

Both Kim and David took a tremendous financial loss when they moved to Virginia. Their bills were just about paid off. They had a house payment that was reasonable. Kim was working part-time at nights. The children were fine and were in a Christian school. The family was going to church but because it was so large, they felt like "little fish in a big pond," and didn't get involved. Kim says that everything was not going well but they were holding their own financially and things were okay when they compared "us to us." But they moved to Virginia and gave up the "bird in the hand" for what David thought was "two in the bush."

The times that Kim thought everything was okay were the times when David was feeling the most stress. It appears there was a connection between the way she was feeling and the way Dave was feeling. If she was content he was unsettled and needed to move.

When they got to Virginia, Kim took a six dollar an hour pay cut and ended up with a part-time job. Dave took a cut in pay to go up there because he thought he would be making bonuses and other benefits, which did not pan out, and he grew more and more miserable. At first they were in an apartment. All the money they had saved and what they had made from the sale of the house in Montgomery was spent paying bills. So, Kim was not happy with this situation at all because she had hoped to use the money to put down on another house. David became very, very depressed. He went to the doctor who prescribed Prozac. This was not the first time David had taken this drug. He had taken it when they lived in Montgomery for what he said was weight loss. Adding this drug to the pain killers he was taking was not good but Kim ignored the danger of it.

He became so depressed that he would sit in front of the TV and watch "The Three Stooges" in the morning before he went to work. Kim and David prayed and tried everything to dig themselves out of this depression. The church to which they were going was not very supportive at all, and they eventually were forced to change churches.

Lately, Kim has been thinking a lot about David and wondering what was on his mind. Looking at pictures that they took on vacation the weekend before he killed himself and the children, she cannot help but think how awful he looked. She said, "He really looked drained out," and she remembers thinking about the state of mind he was in then. She wonders if even then, during what was such a good time for the family, he had determined to do what he did. Of course, she doesn't know. It's so hard to say what was on David's mind.

The Trip To Myrtle Beach

Kim was off for the whole week and David was scheduled to be off Wednesday, Thursday and Friday. They had originally planned to go to Hilton Head, but as it turned out, they stopped at Myrtle Beach because the driving was so tiring. Kim remembers going down there how erratic David was driving. He made her so mad she took over the driving. She said, "Dave, you act like you're running off the road on purpose." Now she wonders if he was taking so many pain killers that he was out of it. He was really odd that whole weekend now that she looks back on it.

When they got to Myrtle Beach, Kim thought they would stay in a motel but they found a nice condo on the beach. Dave went in and Kim and the children stayed in the car while he made the arrangements. He came back to the car and said, "Well, we've got some rooms here," and Kim said, "Here! It looks like it's so expensive." He said, "Don't worry about it. I've taken care of it. We're just going to have a good time this weekend." Kim said, "Okay," and they had a fabulous time compared to their every day hum-drum lifestyle.

The condo in which they stayed was right on the ocean. It was great. Kim had so much fun with the children. She says that it is hard to remember just how David fit in most of the time. Everyone seemed to be in a good mood and relaxed, except for the last night when Dave became restless. Dave ordered pizza one night; another night he took the family to the Dixie Stampede. Dave lied to Kim about how much this cost, and she doesn't really know where he got the money to pay for it. The police told Kim later that sometimes the behavior David exhibited was the precursor to suicide. Suicidal people want to have one last big "blowout" before they end their lives. They just spend all kinds of money and do things they seldom get a chance to do.

On Friday night, Dave was very restless. He tossed and turned, got up and went out to the car in his underwear, and Kim kept thinking, "What is he doing?" Now she wonders if he had hoped he had some drugs hidden somewhere in the car and had gone out to try to find some of them. After the incident of the homicide/suicide, the police found nineteen empty prescription bottles of pain killers. Kim isn't sure what time span the prescriptions covered. I wish now Kim had kept the bottles when the police offered them to her but she didn't and we must try to put this puzzle together without them. Then David came back to bed and just had to have sex. It was like an obsession — he had to do this. There was no love involved. It was just a very aggressive physical act. It's like he just had to do it — it was really strange. Now that Kim looks back on it, his behavior was so bizarre the last few days before he died. I have recently decided, and I tried to convince Kim of this idea, that David was out of drugs and was in withdrawal which caused the unusual behavior.

The family came back home to Virginia on Saturday. Kim remarked how bombed out she was and how she dreaded to go back to work. David never said anything about how he felt or feeling like he wanted to end it all. He was not like Kim's mother. She was always talking about suicide saying things like, "Life wasn't worth living" and "she thought she would go off in the woods and dig a hole and die." Sometimes she would say she was "going off in the woods and dig a hole and eat worms," something crazy like that, or "you'll be better off without me" or those kind of things. Dave never said any of those things. As far as Kim can remember he left no hint whatsoever.

Even though he didn't use death-wish language or anything, he just came more and more unglued. In the last year or so that he lived, David went from one ailment to another. Every time he would get over one thing and Kim would think, "Well, that's it for now. Maybe he'll be well," and he would get something else. If it weren't the toothache, he would fall and get hurt. He would have this surgery and that surgery. I don't know if these illnesses were considered psychosomatic or not because they required medical treatment. One time he fell in a friend's driveway and embedded rocks in his hand and wrist and had to have surgery. He had an appendectomy, a spur removed from his heel and other things.

The episode about the pin in the crackers is just really bizarre. That happened on Monday, exactly one week before the day he died. He called Kim at home because she was on vacation all that week, and said, "You will never believe what just happened. I bit into a cracker and there was a pin it and it stuck in my gum." Kim remembers feeling a little bit disgusted and she said, "David, you are the unluckiest person I've ever seen in my life." The dentist x-rayed it, pulled the pin out, and then David decided he was going to file a claim against the cracker company. He said, "I found a pin in this other cracker," and Kim told him to go have it x-rayed which he did, and sure enough, there was a pin in it. Kim believed him but now looking back, she thinks it was all bogus. I believe it was his passive/aggressive disorder, needing to stick pins in himself in an act of self-mutilation. Kim thinks he planted the pins in the crackers. He invented it. His mind was just going — it was shot. It appears that he thought he was going to get some money from the cracker company. The family was okay financially — tight but not bankrupt. Dave and Kim were not overwhelmed with debt, yet money just seemed to slip through their fingers, and she wonders now if David was going to doctors, getting prescriptions, paying cash, and not charging it to their HMO to avoid getting caught. That's $100.00 for one visit which can destroy any budget. Someone asked Kim if David gambled, but she never saw any evidence of it. She was also asked if he was embezzling money. She never saw any of it if he was. Yet at the last, he got really irritated and paranoid about money and everything else that seemed threatening. Dave and Kim never seemed to come to good terms on how much money to spend on the children. They each had a separate checking account, and she paid her bills and spent most of her money on the children and he paid his. They just sort of got by from week to week.

Kim thinks about it over and over and wonders what in the world was on his mind. How could he have gotten to that point? She has no clue. It's just mind boggling to her to think that suicide was the only solution for him. Not only that, but to think that to kill the children was a solution for them when they didn't have a problem in the world. How *unfair* can things be in this life?

At first Kim was really angry that he didn't get her too. She thought, "Well, why am I left? I'm always left to clean up his mess and that's exactly what I felt. I felt angry with him, obviously, for killing the children. It was such a trauma. It almost killed me anyway and slow death is worse than being shot."

Kim says that what happened was almost in character with David. It was just one more mess to clean up — the final mess he had made. Kim feels so betrayed by him because she always believed in him. She always thought that he had potential and he could really make something of himself. She trusted him and he betrayed that trust.

Being a religious person Kim says she thought of the scripture which says, "Love suffers long; it's kind. It believes the best about someone, always endures, perseveres" and she thinks those are the things she did for David and it seems like love did not win. She loved him as much as she could and it wasn't good enough, and that's the frustrating thing for her. Somehow she believed that if she had just loved him enough, if she had just mothered him enough, there was surely something she could do for him that would turn him around. But he didn't. He just never turned around and you see where it all ended.

Kim thinks that maybe she was trying to remake him, but the last few years of their marriage she really tried to accept him as he was. She just said, "That's David — he's never going to change. I'm not going to try to change him. I'm going to accept him, and I really felt like I was beginning to accept the fact that he was overweight and he was never going to be anything but obese." (At the time he died he weighed 325 pounds and was only 5' 9" tall.) Kim had begun to accept the fact that he had gone as far as he was going in his career, that his estate was worth about as much as he would ever have, and yet that somehow seemed to be okay. Kim felt like she had her children and that was good enough at that time. Her career was going well and she felt like in a few years she could go back to school as soon as the children were out of college and do some things that she wanted to do, career wise. I'm going to encourage her to do that and use her education to help others.

As hard as Kim tried, she was not perfect. She did some things that she feels were really not so good, such as becoming emotionally dependent on men other than her husband to give her what David did not. I am helping Kim work through this.

Kim had been writing to a male friend whom she had known for about ten years. He lived in another city. Because of the nature of their jobs when they worked together, they had a lot of time to talk, and they got really close. She became very dependent on him. He was a Christian and they always tried to keep their relationship on the up and up, but they did have a strong, but controlled attraction for one another.

When Kim's family moved to Virginia, she was so very lonely . . . this man was one of her dearest friends and she began writing to him and he wrote back to her.

David Found Letters

About two months before the homicide/suicide happened, Kim was asleep on the couch and Dave came downstairs. He was as white as a ghost, and he said, "Kim, are you going to leave me?" She said, "No," and he said, "I've found some letters up there. Have you had an affair with this man?" She said, "David, I've not had an affair." I don't know if he believed her or not but she says it's the truth — she did not sleep with this man.

David just couldn't let it go. He kept asking her questions. She said, "David, look, you read those letters. If you see anything sexual in them, you let me know. What you see is what you get." In the letters her friend said that he admired her and wanted things to be good for her. He talked about praying for each other. Kim says, "I know I'm trying to justify it, but I had no close friends up there. David had dragged me off to this strange place where I felt disconnected from everyone. David wasn't meeting my emotional needs and didn't seem interested in trying to. He was not affirming me, and so I wrote to my friend, and he wrote back and we kept in touch. Dave got really upset about that. I'm sure if the shoe had been on the other foot, I would have been upset, too."

All the letters were in a shoe box. Realizing how much they were bothering David, Kim took them to the dumpster and disposed of them. When she told him, he seemed to feel much better. I wish now that she had had David destroy them which might have allowed him to vent some anger symbolically but she didn't know that then and it's too late for hindsight to help.

Kim asked David for forgiveness and he seemed to have forgiven her. They talked about it and she told him that she was overwhelmed with loneliness. She said, "I cannot tell you how many times I've been to bed by myself while you stayed up watching TV, paying no attention to me and I cried myself to sleep." He said, "I've been extremely lonely, too." Kim says that she wishes they had gone to counseling together right then, but they didn't.

David was just totally clueless as to what a marriage was supposed to be. Kim felt like his mama, his maid, everything except a wife. He resented the children and resented her, so she feels like his ultimate temper tantrum was to do what he did. She resents him for it. It's so hard for her to forgive him for being so *unfair.*

Laboring To Forgive

One day Kim is going to have to forgive David and forgive herself. She is working on it but it is hard — really hard. Forgiveness is the place she wants to be. She says that it seems, however, like she's driving in circles and forgiveness is a place that she's just "passing through." Just when she thinks she's there, she begins driving out of town away from forgiveness. She just can't seem to stay there.

Maybe this is why she feels so desperate for answers, or maybe if she could come to an understanding, she could live permanently in the town of forgiveness, or at least stop at a red light for a few minutes. She analyzes, or as I often tell her, she ruminates on everything. It is like having a 5,000 piece jigsaw puzzle halfway complete. It captures you until you make all the pieces fit. Kim says that she feels like that if she gets to piece number 4,500, that the rest of the pieces will be gone and then she wonders if it is worth working so hard to forgive. Her confidants tell Kim she is going to have to learn to live the rest of her life with unanswered questions. She is now convinced that she is going to need God's divine help to teach her how to forgive and maintain forgiveness. As any other person, she only has two choices, to forgive or not to forgive. Kim says, "How can I forgive him when I view the autopsy reports and see what he did to my children? Then I think how can I not forgive him when I compare my son's bloody body on his private bedroom floor with God's Son who was brutalized publicly so that we could forgive and receive forgiveness." Then she prays this prayer, "Lord, God, have mercy on me until I learn to forgive."

Kim further says, "I don't want sympathy. I want understanding. Somehow I need to wipe my slate clean and start over, and I think if it weren't for my children I could have already done that. I'm more mature and much wiser now than I've ever been, but what a hard way to learn such a valuable, but extraordinary lesson."

I think Kim realizes that she can do one of several things: (1) give up and die; (2) be bitter and cynical the rest of her life; (3) become restless, careless and selfish; or, (4) become the caring, compassionate Christian woman that Amy and Eric could be proud of. She says she is committed to becoming that person. She pleads with her friends to "forgive me and feel free to hold up my arms when they become weary in well-doing."

If Kim survives this tragedy, she is going to need the support of her friends for many years to come. I'm not going to be unrealistic and believe that this book will be a panacea for her and cure all the hurts she has endured through the years. Kim is not there but she's moving in the right direction.

68

4

Did Kim See It Coming?

Kim has been asked so many times if she could not see this tragedy coming, and she has asked herself the same question; it's always there. She wonders now if she should have tried to suppress David's fascination with Civil War battles, the old vintage, pearl-handled gun, or his obvious addiction to pain killers. Had she been infinitely tolerant of a less than perfect person to whom she was married, or had she learned to focus on the children and ignore David? Kim says, "I now ask myself: Where were my boundaries? Why was my tolerance of David's drug use without limits? Should I have paid closer attention to his agitation and taken my children out of a dangerous situation? Now, in light of what happened, I know I should have done something — but what? I just didn't see it coming or I would have attempted to prevent it."

When pressed about David's overuse of pain killers, she says, "He was functioning, going to work and I just took for granted that it was all right for him to have the drugs if it kept him happy."

Kim honestly feels that she didn't see signs that would culminate in such an unimaginable end to the only world that she knew. In hindsight, as she tries to reconstruct the relationship her husband had with his children, she can see some agitation building between Eric and his father. David seemed to have adored Amy and she did him. There was an adversarial division developing in their family. The obvious power struggle seemed to worsen as Eric's emotional level pulled even with, and at times, surpassed that of his father. David and Eric were not always kind to one another, and Kim became the mediator between them. She can't suppress the thought that they probably had had an argument before David killed him. Several weeks before the 17th of July, David had ranted and raved with Eric until Eric was crying and saying, "Why does my daddy hate me?"

As Kim looks back, she can see how awkward it had become for David to adjust to two little children suddenly becoming young adults. They were beginning to discern the maternal organization of their family. Apparently there was more discomfort in David's mind, knowing that his children had begun to ignore him as the family leader, than Kim could have calculated.

Is Kim Responsible?

The death of a child is a parent's worst nightmare. The more dependent the child is on the parent, the greater the responsibility seems to be. Even though the ages of Amy and Eric put them at a time in their lives that would lessen Kim's custodial responsibility, the way the deaths happened seemed to make her feel as responsible for them as if she had been careless with her protection and personally created their peril. I don't want to make Kim seem self-righteous but it was not like she was driving a car in which they were killed, or carelessly set the house on fire. She didn't feed them contaminated food or let them drown in an unguarded pool. As far as she knows she didn't do anything. I've asked her to say, "David did it — I didn't." She didn't see it coming.

I'm sure with more time and therapy Kim will come to accept the fact that she had nothing to do with their deaths, and that there was nothing, conscious or unconscious, that she could have done to David to make him violate his conscience and kill his children. That was his decision, as warped as it seems to have been, and his actions were probably due to a mental disorder that destroyed his reasoning power.

Deep down in her heart Kim knows that if she had seen any signs she would have prevented it, even if it meant giving her life. Kim says, "I know they are empty words to say you would give your life for another person because it is an untested commitment, but as much as lieth in me I believe I would have killed or been killed to have saved my children."

Did God Warn Kim?

Being a religious person, Kim feels strongly at times that if God had loved her like He should have, He would have warned her of this impending tragedy in a way that she could not have misunderstood so that she could have protected her children. Kim said, "And, I must add, I would have tried to prevent David from killing himself even if the children had not been involved. I felt very protective of him and I often mothered him like I did the children, a mistake I am determined never to repeat."

Where was Kim's intuition, or her maternal radar that was supposed to sense impending danger in her children's lives? I have guided Kim through some of these questions by helping her understand that it is unrealistic to believe that we can always know what others are thinking. God, in His infinite wisdom, chose to create us with the ability to make our own decisions. With this in mind, she accepts the fact that she didn't make up David's mind about much of what he did in life. As strong as she was, she was still compliant in most cases. He made the choice to kill his children and he did not include her in whatever process he used to make that idiotic decision.

Kim says, "It's frightening to think that we could have lived together for eighteen years, had two children, just been on a wonderful vacation, and David could have destroyed my whole family in such a 'no-brainer' way. I had no idea, not one discernible clue, that it was going to happen. No! I didn't see it coming."

Not one person has ever blamed Kim for what David did.

She has no reason to be defensive and I have not allowed her to be. In the questioning phase of her grief, she blamed herself without any rationale, but I took care of her guilt in a swift and forceful way, sparing her the unnecessary guilt and shame that she could have suffered.

If she could recall some small clue that David had tried to give her, she would be glad to take whatever responsibility she deserves, but she just did not see it coming. If she had any warning she would have never gone to work that day. I have come to know Kim quite well and she is the type person who would have devised a way to stop the tragedy if she had seen it coming.

Kim Had Some Afterthoughts

Kim, some time after the tragic event, began thinking about the odd things that transpired a couple of months before July 17, that in retrospect, could have been interpreted as warning signs. It almost seemed to her like there were things that crossed her mind that made her think about what life would be like if she didn't have David and the children. For instance, one time she was cleaning the bathroom and she thinks that she kept wondering about what she would do if she didn't have anyone to clean up after.

Another time she thinks that she remembers wondering about David's hands and she thought, "What would I ever do if I never saw him again, if I never held his hands again? You can call it coincidence, premonition, or whatever you want to, but those are thoughts that I had a couple of months before that infamous day."

Kim believes she had these thoughts but it is highly possible that these were products of the trauma she experienced.

Kim's Vision

While she was praying one day, Kim had an image of having a wound in her chest that reached from one side to the other. She remembers saying to God, "Please, God, don't let it be the kids." She adds, "You can call that premonition, coincidence, wondering imagination, or whatever you want to, but it is strange that I would have these thoughts, especially in light of the tragedy that happened." Again I caution, these could be fall-outs from the trauma Kim suffered.

Where Was God?

Kim is not a theologian and what she has to say comes from her emotional rather than her rational side. Her family was church-going, God-fearing people. They were in no wise religious fanatics. Their style of worship was quiet and personal. None of them, with the exception of Amy, were highly visible church workers, but they did participate in some of the activities of church life and were not alienated from God by any stretch of the imagination.

Though Kim was not perfect and had made many mistakes, at no time did she feel that she had committed some egregious sin and that God was punishing her by the death of her children. Conversely, she believed that she was a good person, loving mother, supportive wife, and thought that she should have been rewarded with blessings, not punitive vengeance.

Maybe the Psalmist's claim that "those who sow in tears shall reap in joy" holds more promise for her, but right now she would give up any joy for the return of her children. Kim says, "In my irrational moments I almost believe that God could send my babies back if He wanted to, but when I'm not in intense grief and thinking rationally, I know it's not His nature to do so. Perhaps this thinking fostered some of the dreams I shall discuss later."

Kim has had trouble admitting how angry she was with God for letting this happen to her. I suggested to her that her anger was indicative of her faith in God's omnipotence rather than believing that He was personally responsible for her children's deaths. She does believe, however, that if David had followed the will of God, they all, father and children, would still be alive. She believes that God did not want David to be so twisted as to have killed his children and himself. She knows that it was not God's will that her children should perish at the hands of their father. Their deaths, and the manner in which they died, were far from the nature of a loving God.

I also suggested that Kim's human predicament was analogous to that of Job, the biblical character who lost his family and possessions much like she did. Ancient Job wanted to know where God was just as Kim did on July 17, 1995, when she discovered her children had been killed. Job had been a good person, faithful to God in every way. He was not aware that God had bargained with Satan to try to break his faith.

After discussing this with Kim, she said, "May I say to God, Satan almost broke my faith, but he didn't. God, I know where you are and I know where Amy and Eric are. Please, by your grace, let me be there, too."

Twenty-four hours before he died, Eric had said that he wanted to go to heaven and wanted Kim to go there, too. She had no idea that it would be so soon. Kim says, "I certainly don't believe Eric felt that his dad was going to kill him and that he was going to heaven the next day. It could have been a coincidence, but in hindsight, it does make one think when tragic things like that happen. I'm sure God knew it, but I didn't. However, I do want to go to heaven."

5 The Funerals

I had Kim to make a tape about the funerals and I also listened to the funeral message. I let Kim tell part of the story and then I edited the rest of it. Kim said that the thing I most remember about the funerals is that I was still in shock when all the arrangements had to be made. The day that it happened I didn't want to call anyone or make any preparations. I felt like if I could just go to sleep and wake up, it would just be a bad dream. That evening, friends started making the necessary arrangements for me and the news began to spread. Then I knew it was all true.

If numbness is an emotion, I

suppose that is the description of how I felt. I felt like all these things were happening on a movie screen to someone else whom I didn't even know. It really hadn't dawned on me that it was my family that was dead. I had not cried at all that day until someone asked me what to do with Amy's puppy that we had just given to her a couple of weeks before. When I turned around and saw Shiloh, I just broke down and couldn't stop crying. I kept thinking how could Amy be gone and the puppy still be here. It just didn't make any sense and I cried and cried after that simple incident. I was to learn later that the simplest things could trigger my tears.

The next day I had to begin to make funeral arrangements. I wanted my family to be buried in Alabama but I wanted a service in Virginia, too, so we had two services. After the service in Virginia, their bodies were shipped back to Birmingham, Alabama, for a service where they would be buried.

David's older brother came up from Birmingham and helped me with the arrangements for which I will always be thankful. We picked out the caskets and planned a suitable service. The funeral director was absolutely wonderful. He was very sensitive, loving and deeply moved by the whole thing. At times, when he was talking to me, he would become choked up and teary. He made all of the arrangements to have the bodies shipped to Alabama, everything down to the last detail. We stayed in close contact before the funeral. He told me specific details as to what had to be done, who needed to be contacted, what to do about the autopsies, and what reports had to be gathered. I cannot speak of him highly enough because he really helped me through a very difficult time.

After the arrangements were made, it came time to view the bodies. It was one of the most difficult things I have ever had to do in my entire life.

The funeral home was in an antique-looking building in an old section of town. My very best girlfriend from Montgomery, and David's brother and his wife were with me. We were first escorted into a small parlor where we sat for a short while. David's parents and my dad were not ready to view the bodies yet, so we decided to go ahead and view them since it would not be long before others would be coming in.

It was hard to go in where they were. They were in a little chapel which was set up with David on the left, Amy in the middle, and Eric on the right. They were playing soft organ music and the chapel smelled with flowers. I remember walking down the hallway to the chapel with my head buried in my girlfriend's arms. She was holding me up and I was crying my heart out.

When we got to the caskets, I looked at David and he didn't even look like himself. He was so swollen and artificial looking. Because no one was supposed to go back in the house, I asked my neighbors to go to the clothing store to buy clothes for David, Amy and Eric to wear for their burial. They had chosen a dark pair of pants and a white shirt and tie for David. Amy had a blue printed dress. When I first saw it, before they took it to the funeral home, I thought, "that will be so pretty on her." Then I realized she was dead. The neighbors chose a white shirt and tie and some jeans for Eric.

Then I looked at my little Amy and she was all puffed and swollen and didn't look like herself. I looked at Eric and he looked the most like himself. He had his little hand lying across his body in a natural pose and I thought, "Well, I'll just touch his hand and everything will be okay." When I touched his hand, instead of it being warm and alive like I had expected, it was cold. At that point, I ran out of the chapel and began to beat my fist against the wall saying, "Why did he do this? Why did he do this? Why did he do this?" I was just hysterical.

After I calmed down, my sister-in-law said, "Kim, we're not going through this again." So, at that point, we decided not to open the caskets again. Some of our friends were disappointed because they didn't get to see the children one last time. It was my choice and I couldn't deal with looking at them. They had to accept not seeing the bodies the best way they could. I know that saying "good-bye" is a great part of closure, but at the time I couldn't handle seeing them in such an unnatural state.

The minister at the church in Virginia talked me through a lot of things and allowed me to discuss what kind of service I wanted. I wanted it to be a service of hope, to be special and meaningful, and it turned out to be that way. We sang Amy's favorite song, "I'll Fly Away". The minister said some wonderful things about the children and some very comforting things about David.

The Virginia Service

Three copper-colored caskets formed a T-shape at the front

of the auditorium. Atop each casket was a single red rose laced in baby's breath — baby's breath — strange that baby's breath covered the coffins of my babies who now had no breath in them. Those three caskets were all that remained of the loving family I had adored. They held all my hopes and dreams, all my memories, my past, my present, and what I thought would be my future. Now all those things would soon be buried in the ground. How could all that I knew of life and loved so much be swept away in an instant leaving me with nothing? How could this me?

The church in Virginia was filled with my friends and co-workers who gave me such comforting support. The friends of Eric and Amy were filled with compassion and were truly grieved themselves. I had no idea how much this affected them until someone told me that a counselor was brought to the church to help the kids in the youth group deal with this.

There were two receiving lines, one at the beginning of the service and one at the end. Both times I was the "consolee" and the "consoler." The teenagers brought me flowers and pictures of their latest church trip. One of Amy's friends offered to adopt her puppy. She had been saving her money to buy a puppy and her dad had already built a fence, so she took Shiloh. I am glad that one of Amy's good friends is taking care of her puppy.

The service was conducted by one of the associate ministers of the church in Virginia. These were his words about each member of Kim's family, beginning with Amy.

The Eulogies
Amy

Amy was sensitive to the needs of people and that made her like a magnet in a crowd. Kim was telling me about Amy returning from a church tour full of stories of helping people and the fresh experience of sharing her faith through music and drama. She had a sweet personality. If you knew Amy, you would have known it was easy to talk to her and you just wanted to put your arms around her and hug her. She had a gentle spirit that endeared her to her neighbors, teachers and her peers. In fact, the school counselor told Kim, even this morning, that Amy had recently received the first "Random Act of Kindness" award. I think that speaks of her spirit.

Amy volunteered her time to work in Vacation Bible School at her neighbor's church where she was loved and adored by the children. In fact, the minister of that church told me how anxious he was to have her come back this year and work.

She had a desire to be a veterinarian because of her love for animals. This past year Amy had been baptized into the family of faith. One of the church tour sponsors said that Amy was very serious about her faith and was growing in Christ.

Eric

Eric was an honor student. If you ever knew him, you found out very quickly that he was quiet, studious and very lovable. One of his Bible study teachers and I talked this afternoon and she said that Eric was always raising his hand to answer questions in class. Even though he was shy, he was always ready to give a lovable, friendly hug.

Even when Eric was much younger, he expressed himself in a most articulate fashion through his poetry for which he won several awards. He enjoyed playing the guitar and was beginning to gain some confidence in his ability to play.

Eric was intuitive and wanted to become an engineer. He had a great curiosity to figure out things and saw life as a challenge, asking poignant questions about the world and about his faith.

Kim mentioned that recently she had had to have a loving conversation with Eric about his tongue and the tone of voice that he was using. She said she had forgotten about the incident, and a few days later, as she was sorting clothes to be laundered, she noticed a piece of paper in one of Eric's pants pockets. She was not trying to be nosy but she opened up the piece of paper and it was a list of scriptures about the use of the tongue. He had used his concordance to do the study — that's how studious he was.

You see, Eric, too, had a growing faith. He loved the Bible. He learned the Word of God, and in his own adolescent faith, he was in the process of living by it. One of the books that he had been reading was *Life on the Edge* by Dr. James Dobson — a very challenging, very intellectual book for a young man of his age to be reading but that says who Eric was.

David

David was a fun-loving, friendly, many times known as an "everybody's buddy" kind of guy. He helped people and cared for them. Kim told me the other day, with a smile on her face, that that was what had attracted her to him.

In the grand lobby of our church building, David would maneuver his way through the crowd to shake my hand or to visit with one of the other ministers. That seemed to be a real point of affirmation for him.

I remember one day we were just talking casually and I said, "David, now tell me again where you are from?" He said, "L. A." I said, "Los Angeles?" He said, "No, Lower Alabama." That just summarizes his sense of humor and wit. David, just as Amy and Eric, had confessed his faith in Christ and was baptized.

The Sermon

The minister preached on the subject of *God's Inseparable Love*. He said of all the sorrows that we can experience, there is none quite so difficult as when one has taken his own life. Family and friends alike are not only left to suffer all of the normal emotions that accompany the loss of a loved one, we are also left with unanswered questions. We wonder, Why did this happen? Were there any signals that should have been seen? Did we offer all the love and support that we could have offered? Could we have done anything different to prevent the circumstances that took place this week?

To be honest, there are no simple answers to that complex question. That makes this experience, as a minister and for you as a congregation, so difficult to endure.

Our only hope in a time like this is to look to God for strength, comfort and peace, for He has promised us that nothing can separate us from His love.

The minister read from Romans 8:35-39 where Paul penned the expression of inseparable love. He actually began with verse 28 which says, . . . in all things God works for the good of those that love Him, who are called according to His purpose.

He said the Bible doesn't say that those who love God never suffer difficulty or have conflict in their lives, but it says that for all those who love the Lord and are called according to His purpose, all things work together for good.

Then he read verses 35-39 where Paul asked the question: Who shall separate us from the love of Christ? The minister went on to say that these words, perhaps more than any others penned, express the basis of our hope and our comfort in this time of sorrow and grief.

His sermon consisted of three points. The first is that God has an *astounding* love for us. All the way from Genesis to Revelation, there is a message of love. God says in Jeremiah 31:3, I have loved you with an everlasting love. In John 3:16, he says He loved the world so much that He gave His only begotten Son, that whosoever would believe in Him would not perish but would experience everlasting love.

Further God says in John, No greater love has any man ever shown but that he would lay down his life for his friends. We understand how God might ignore us, or how He might even condemn us, but how could He love us with such astounding love, when we are all sinful?

The minister warned that it is easy for us to categorize sin and say that one sin is greater than another, but in the eyes of God, sin is sin. Anything that separates us from God is sin.

Someone has said that the mountains are God's love piled high. The oceans are God's love spread out and the flowers are God's love in bloom, but the purest expression of God's love is found in the cross. Paul declares in Romans 5:6-8, When we were yet without strength (and I want to put a parenthesis around that, which means, powerless to save ourselves) in due time, Christ died for the ungodly.

The minister addressed Kim and others, and said, "Kim, family and friends, in our sorrow, don't forget God's love is inseparable, and He loves us personally."

His second point was that God's love is *surrounding* because it covers every circumstance of life and nothing can separate us from it. Things may separate us from health or wealth, family and friends, comfort and from ease, but they cannot separate us from the love of Christ.

The minister exhorted the audience not to judge David unless they were willing to judge their own lives because everyone misses the mark. He said that people get right in the face of a pure, righteous and Holy God, and sin, yet they categorize sin, put it in a little box with a bow on it, and say that his is the worst sin and God can never forgive that. If that be the case, then God can forgive none of us because we are all unrighteous, impure and unholy. We will do irrational things and make poor decisions that will have terrible consequences but He will still love us.

His last point was that it is an *abounding* love because we don't need to be overcome, whipped or defeated by our circumstances, but we can be overcomers through Him. God gives us grace to stand up to life and supplies inner braces for the outer pressures that we experience. The greatest enemies that we face are sin, suffering and death, but through Christ we can have victory over sin by His death, victory over suffering through His presence, and victory over death through His resurrection.

As Paul declares in I Timothy 1:10, He hath abolished death. In other words, Christ has rendered it powerless and brought life and immortality to light through His gospel.

He told the story about Walter Winchell, a famous radio news commentator during World War II, who after a particularly dark week during which the Port of Singapore fell, closed his broadcast with this sentence: "Singapore has fallen but the Rock of Ages stands."

You probably feel as though your world has fallen in this week. That's the way I've felt at different times, but God reminds us that the Rock of Ages still stands. Christ lives, loves, lifts, strengthens, and sustains us if we will look to Him and recognize that nothing can separate us — even ourselves — from the love of God.

The minister closed with this: Eric had been reading a book by Dr. James Dobson which is about the struggles we face in life — grief, discouragement, pain, anxiety, and loneliness. The chapter that really got Eric's attention tells the story about "Pistol" Pete Maravich, the great basketball player of LSU, who broke all the collegiate scoring records and was kind of the pacesetter, the trendsetter, the flash of professional basketball. He was inducted into the Basketball Hall of Fame the first time he was eligible.

Dobson and Pete were playing some pick-up basketball in the gym, and after it was over, Maravich fell to the floor. Dobson thought it was a joke because Pete had been talking about being out of shape, but when he approached him, he saw Pete going into convulsions and right there in his arms, "Pistol" Pete Maravich died at the age of forty. On Pete's tee shirt that day was inscribed, "Looking Unto Jesus". He had experienced riches, fame and glory, but his life had been radically transformed and he was now looking unto Jesus.

Dobson said that he was so burdened he went home, sat down with his son, looked him in the eye and said, "Son, I've got to tell you something today that is heavy on my heart. The most important decision you'll ever make is having a relationship with Jesus. It's important that I know that when you go before the Lord, you'll be there with me. Don't let anything deter you and I'll be there at that eastern gate to meet you."

Eric told Kim, "Mom, that grabbed my heart. I want to

be there. I want you to be there. I want Amy and Dad to be there, and my friends to be there."

The minister said that he and one of the student interns went over to Wendy's to get a sandwich that afternoon before the funeral and there were two men talking about the events of this week. One of the men said, "You know, preachers are dumb and they don't really have a clue about what's going on in life."

He then added, But I tell you this is one preacher that has gotten a good handle on what's going on in life this week. There are a lot of hurting people and I would venture to say there are some hurting people in this room tonight.

If it takes three caskets to get some of you to ask what adjustments you need to make or how you need to look at some things differently, then this tragedy will not have happened in vain.

The Second Funeral

When Kim was on the plane flying from Virginia to Birmingham for the second funeral, she looked out of the window, saw the clouds and began to think, "Just like the song says, my children have flown away. They have joined Jesus in the clouds." She was wondering if they could see her and tried to imagine what heaven would be like. I told Kim that almost always when a child dies, we think "gone to be an angel", whether that's theologically correct or not. Such a thought brought much comfort to Kim's aching heart.

The circumstances of the funeral in Birmingham were

totally different from the one in Virginia. It was extremely hard for Kim to go through two funerals for her children and her husband in such a brief time period; therefore, the second service was anti-climatic and I doubt if it's fair to compare the two. She was not as impressed with the funeral director as she had been with the one in Virginia. He seemed very cold and business-like. The funeral home where the funeral was held did not please her. It was cold and sterile and had a morgue atmosphere. The Birmingham arrangements were made very quickly by David's family, and even though they did their best, she is not happy with where they are buried. The cemetery is in a bad part of town and she's not comfortable going there by herself, something she needs to do for her healing process.

The funeral service itself was meaningful. She remembers the minister saying, "Kim, it's almost as if you can hear the brush of angels' wings as they come to hold you up, and busy themselves getting you through this day."

Kim says she remembers sitting there looking at the coffins. Amy's had pink flowers on it. She kept thinking, "Amy, you would have a fit if you knew there were pink flowers on your grave." She always fussed about things being in pink and Kim chuckled to herself as she could see Amy's reactions to those pink flowers.

Kim was getting very depressed by this time and suddenly she felt like the children were speaking to her. They were saying, "Mom, come on now, you know this is not us in these coffins." Right then and there Kim felt an inner peace. She said,

"I don't know whether the words came from them or just my own imagination." While they were alive the children were always trying to take care of Kim so she felt like this continued after they were dead. But Kim felt like "that's true; they are not in there in those caskets. They're in heaven with Jesus and everything is going to be good for them forever. They're safe in the arms of Jesus." Kim's friends say they remember how serene she looked at the funeral and that there was an aura of peacefulness about her.

Kim told me, "I didn't want a lot of uncontrolled crying. I wanted dignity for my family. It was all I could do to get through that service without bursting into uncontrolled grief."

There was a short graveside committal service. One scripture was read, the minister prayed, and it was over. The scripture was one that Kim had chosen from Habakkuk 3:17-19. Kim had that read because she wanted people to know that she believes that in the emptiness of such times, God is still there for us. Though she has been angry with God, wrestled with Him on many occasions after the death of her family, rebelled against Him, and shaken her fist in His face, He has been there for her and she knows that God was the only thing holding her up at the second funeral.

6 | Why Did David Do It?

Suicide

When David chose to take his and the children's lives, his family and friends not only experienced loss, but they faced a lot of unanswered questions. Suicide is a very complex human behavior and we as survivors will probably never know why David chose to end his life and kill his children.

Kim and I have decided not to dwell extensively on suicide but to have another book forthcoming on the subject. Kim says that on the evening of the terrible tragedy of July 17, 1995, she had not yet told anyone exactly what had happened. All they knew was that David and the children had been shot, so when David's parents arrived, they all came into the bedroom of Kim's neighbor's house where she was staying and asked immediately if they had any idea who had done it. Kim said, "Well, we need to talk about it. It looks like David did this." They were all devastated and grasping for reasons, just some little point of reference on which to hold, but at the time there was no obvious reason for such an unreasonable act.

David's brother and his wife felt like they could find a reason and they went to the house and checked everything, gathered up the bills, and that sort of thing. They thought for sure that something was terribly wrong that had forced David over the edge. Kim and David were tight financially but they were not in debt over their heads. Apparently, things were okay at David's work. He had not embezzled money or anything as far as they could tell.

There is still no concrete evidence of anything being so grossly wrong that David would do what he did, but Kim has implored me to help her understand why David did it. I told her that generally speaking people commit suicide when they are more afraid of the consequences of living than they are of dying. Suicide is a very selfish act and seldom takes other people's feelings into consideration. Those who contemplate self-destruction have turned their total concern toward themselves and their pain or disease (disease should be spelled "dis-ease".) People who commit suicide are usually so filled with anxiety that they feel like misfits socially and suffer biologically because of the stress. When such states of discomfort persist for long periods of time, it becomes mental illness, thus it is considered abnormal. Suicide is abnormal and is the most senseless, and often preventable, cause of death. It is against humankind's basic nature. When all the crows are flying south and one is flying north, the lone crow needs to find out why, because sometimes mental illness or abnormal behavior can run counter to one's own belief system as well as the social norms. A person can lose the ability to cope with normal life experiences and the ability to adjust to life changes becomes faulty. The capacity for happiness and the knowledge of how to maintain happy, fulfilling relationships are deficient. Life is dominated by fear and dread and one's outlook on life is hopeless and he or she has no purpose for living. All possibilities for good seem to escape his or her view of the future and this leads to psychological disorders. The next step is to seek help or eliminate the context of the pain by committing suicide.

Suicide is the tenth leading cause of death in the United States. Around one hundred people in the United States commit suicide every day. This would be higher if there were ways to know the true causes of some accidents which are suicides carefully disguised. Men often choose a violent form of death but women are more inclined to use sleeping pills or something that they think isn't painful. Twice as many men accomplish suicide as women even though more women attempt to take their lives. Some recent figures show this ratio to be five women to every one man who attempts suicide.

There are several general reasons why people commit suicide: sudden change in status, becoming self-centered, thinking society will be better off without them, seeking release from pain, and mental illness.

In David's case, he fit so many of the suicide profile. He was depressed and felt very unhealthy. As Kim expressed to him a week before he died, he was unlucky. Possibly he felt that he was losing the children and her. Career-wise, he was going nowhere and was bored with his work. More and more David was fascinated with Civil War battles. He said while visiting a Civil War cemetery at Gettsyburg, "By next July, I'll be in a place like this." On July 17th of that year he killed himself. The obvious overuse of prescription drugs, overeating, and possibly some other self-destructive behaviors made him vulnerable to suicide.

David had been taking a controversial anti-depressant drug called Prozac that was rumored to cause some people to do unusual things like commit suicide or homicide. Kim later felt like that was the cause and she asked her doctor what he thought about it and he said that there was nothing to the rumor that this medication caused that kind of behavior. She gave the information to an attorney and she looked into it but never got back to her which Kim interpreted to mean that she did not feel like there was enough evidence for a case.

Kim can make some sense out of Dave's past behavior but now nothing else makes sense. Sometimes God doesn't make sense to her. Her behavior doesn't make sense. The world doesn't make sense. Life doesn't make sense. No one, and absolutely no one, can help her make sense out of a senseless act like David killing his children.

I told Kim up front that it was *unfair* and it didn't make any sense. I didn't promise her anything but to help her face the reality of her loss, and to help her take charge of her grief, to let it flow like a river and to help her keep it in the banks. Kim said, "At times the crazy things that have happened to me almost caused me to flood beyond the banks of my sanity, but somehow I have managed to be like 'Ole Man River -- I just keep rolling along."

Depression

No one will ever know why David did what he did. It is helpful to list a few of the things that came out in counseling with Kim about which he might have been depressed: an emotionally unhealthy childhood, obesity, physical and mental health, addictive behavior, obsession with Civil War battles, and fear of failure. David had convinced himself that he was losing Kim because he had found some letters from a male friend of hers. He felt like he was a failure in his career and he knew that Kim wanted to move back to Alabama. In his mind he felt that he couldn't face his friends there. He felt like he was about to get in trouble with the law for purchasing too many pain killers. Five percent of those who suffer from such depression do commit suicide.

There is evidence that Kim and Eric were also depressed. The latest information about depression is that if you live with someone who is depressed, you have a four to six times greater chance of being depressed yourself. If you are married to a depressed person, you have a nine times greater chance of being depressed. Depression breeds depression and can affect the whole family. As more people in the family become depressed, the changes of getting over depression lessens.

As we studied the two major categories of depression, Kim thinks she can see David moving from the simple chronic depression state to an agitated state, especially the Friday and Sunday nights before he committed suicide. He had begun to have such painful thought patterns. His body movements had become slow and deliberate, often sitting in one place watching television for hours. Then without any overt provocation, he would become restless and agitated, suspicious of his boss or co-workers, and even his family and became afraid of the police. He would counter Kim's interest in returning to Alabama with comments like, "I don't think I could face my friends back in Alabama." Kim is not sure what he really meant by that. He could have felt like their move to Virginia was supposed to be seen by his friends as an upward move and to give it up and return would be coming home in defeat. It crushes Kim to think how he returned in sheer defeat and in the worse state of disgrace anyone could ever experience.

Kim is not willing at this point to discount this unfair tragedy and hold no one responsible. That's not healthy for her. Whatever she's done wrong, she must bear the responsibility, pay the price when possible, and forgive herself. She feels that only God can hold David responsible. She finds some consolation in knowing that God's judgment is fair, even if David's actions weren't.

Kim says, "If this had happened to someone else, I'm

sure I would have forgotten it by now since it's been over a year. I haven't forgotten it and I probably never will. It is getting better and I'm not as angry with David as I was. I'm beginning to accept the fact that it might help to understand that some things never make sense. Some things aren't fair in life, like a baby being born severely handicapped, or a father killing his children."

David's Behavior

No matter how angry Kim is, she does not wish to vilify David. With my help she has come to believe that as he pulled the trigger of the 38 revolver, there was no malicious reasoning that caused a dastardly act of a father against his children.

In order to accept the fact that David could have had one or more personality disorders, Kim really wanted to know more about them. As I explained the different disorders to her, I cautioned her that I was not a forensic expert. Also, she should not use one or two symptoms such as David's joking or clowning around to avoid problems or his depression, but to look at in-grained patterns of behavior. We now know that along with other things, David had a very addictive behavior and was afraid of being exposed.

Kim related a story of how one evening in May she had come home from a Tupperware party and David met her at the door, pale and shaking like a leaf. She said, "David, what in the world is wrong with you?" He acted like a little boy and said, "I think I'm in trouble with the law." Kim said, "What do you mean you're in trouble with the law?" David said, "The druggist went to fill my prescription and he said that he was not about to give me any more pain killers and that he was going to call the police." Of course, Kim took David's side and was angry with the pharmacist. Kim said that she doesn't think David ever got over that scared feeling.

Over the years Kim had said, "Well, that's just Dave doing his thing," or "that's just more of Dave's shenanigans". We all have a personality that's unique. The word personality comes from the word "persona" which means mask. We all wear a mask that allows others to identify us. That's our personality.

When Kim looked in retrospect at the overall maladaptive behavior patterns presented by David, it overshadowed the idea that toward the last he was just coming unglued. There was a pattern of passivity. He really was a very angry person most of the eighteen years he and Kim were married but he chose to deal with it in a passive way. Kim knew he was angry with her but she didn't realize that it caused him to withhold emotional support or move every time she began to put down roots. Passive people often get even by withholding emotional support from their spouses, blaming them for it and momentarily becoming very aggressive.

Now that David has killed himself and the children, it is evident that he had a full-blown personality disorder. He seemed to enjoy obstructing Kim's personal growth — procrastinating, complaining, criticizing people in authority without a bonified reason. Most of the time his aggression was unconscious.

Kim believes David was angry with his parents because

of their instability, especially his mother who refused to deal with an alcoholic husband. David was never sure that he was loved by anyone. When first married, Kim had so many reservations about her love for him. I'm sure it was evident from time to time. Then after about two years of marriage, Kim's unconscious hesitancy to establish real intimacy and his doubt about being loved began to take a heavy toll on him.

Airing all of this helps Kim because one of her favorite books, *Telling Yourself the Truth*, taught her to accept the real problems (guilt) in life and separate them from the false or unreal ones. When someone does something as drastic as David did, there is evidence that there was a real problem and she needs to know what it was.

We looked at David's behavior even years before he killed the children. Kim was trying to understand more about David's personality to satisfy the accurate perception phase of her counseling. She was trying to get the big picture of what really happened. I believed it was a part of Kim's healing process and I soon found myself absorbed in trying to piece together David's past behaviors. Kim said, "I guess I would have felt better if the autopsy had revealed a brain tumor or some answers other than a personality disorder. They are somewhat complicated and make it harder to understand. Although I am angry with David for doing such a sinister thing, and feel that his act was directed toward me more than toward the children, I still want to know what pushed him over the edge."

Kim, having a Master's level counseling degree herself,

had a greater need to explore all of the possibilities as to what personality disorders David had that she should have picked up.

As Kim and I explored David's behavior, we looked at several disorders that could have led to suicide. I realize that some of this information seems very technical but because it was a part of the therapeutic process, I have chosen to write it.

Explosive Disorder

Because of David's volatile temper there at the last, we first explored a disorder called Explosive Disorder. This personality disorder is suspected when the person who is suffering from it has occasional uncontrolled bursts of rage. They usually are very docile individuals until they explode. One day they can be the life of the party and the next day demonstrate social withdrawal. Their calmness is a facade for the raging feeling which can erupt like a volcano. They mask their feelings of helplessness and weakness. Like David, they are overly dependent and need mothering which Kim often gave him when he had temper tantrums. This type personality has latent potential of destruction, suicide and murder.

This disorder or behavior often has a neurological basis and can be recorded by an EEG. These individuals usually have been abused or rejected by their parents. Some parents reinforce this behavior by being overly tolerant of their child's outburst of temper.

Some of the characteristics of this disorder did fit David especially the lack of a healthy mode by which to act out his aggressive impulses, a constant high level of anxiety, there at the last. Other characteristics were his obvious addiction to food, prescription drugs, fear of impotency (which he occasionally had), and his feelings of depression and non-achievement on his jobs. He eventually denigrated himself to the point of no self-respect and no self-control, but Kim and I don't think the explosive personality disorder or behavior totally fits David's character.

Passive/Aggressive Personality Disorder

The disorder that most likely fits David was a severe Passive/Aggressive Personality. One reason Kim and I put some stock in this possibility is that the end result for a passive/aggressive male, if untreated, is often suicide. They may use hypochondriac ailments as ways to escape the responsibilities of life which have, in their minds, become overbearing. David was a true hypochondriac. He needed excessive nurturance, and could not tolerate criticism such as job performance reviews and more especially from Kim or the children. In retrospect, Kim feels they were directly or indirectly critical of him. This type personality has a lack of adaptive skills which fit David to a tee. People suffering from this type personality disorder can be the life of the party on the social level. On the interpersonal level, they struggle to establish satisfying relationships. This leaves them with a craving for acceptance and satisfaction. Unfulfilled needs are most often met by overeating and addiction to substance abuse such as the pain killers and other drugs David used. As we've already mentioned in another chapter, David battled a life-long weight problem, being from 100 to 150 pounds overweight.

I know Kim is biased with this particular assessment but I think she feels that David never had her personal interest at heart. This was demonstrated by his demands for her to work full-time and his unwillingness to baby-sit the children. He never seemed to understand her emotional needs but only sought to satisfy his needs. There were times when he seemed to think up ways to get large sums of money, such as the incident of the pins in the crackers. He never felt like he should be responsible for the total support of his family, even though he always held a job.

Probably the final characteristic that caused us to gravitate to the Passive/Aggressive Disorder was David's insecurity. He had an overbearing need for Kim to reassure him that he was loved and his low tolerance for frustration hit rock bottom when he found the letters that Kim received from a male friend from another state.

Passive/Aggressive husbands usually need their wives to lead the family. Mothers are forced to dominate the home, often taking responsibility for the children and the finances for household expenses. This leads to a relationship punctuated with periods of frustration. The husband can vacillate between being angry with his wife for dominating him and requiring more attention or mothering. Anger can manifest itself in an explosion of such magnitude that emotional abuse or physical harm is inflicted on one or more of the family members. This leads to shame and a need for self-mutilation. It was evident that David increasingly took his frustration out on Eric when they had their heated discussions.

When we discussed these disorders, Kim felt that it was so *unfair*. She wonders why in the world David didn't get the treatment he needed for his personality disorders. If he knew he was damaged, why did he wait until they resulted in his death and the death of her children? And, she confesses it almost killed her. She got treatment, but David didn't. It's so *unfair*.

Passive/Aggressive people can reach a point where they yearn for a blissful solution to their emotional pain. At times they can regress to a very immature, emotional age. If they have religious connections, they can find comfort in fantasizing about going to heaven where all their pain will be over. I personally think this is what David was thinking when he killed himself and the children. The peace and tranquillity of the beach increased this fantasy if indeed that's what was on his mind.

Anti-Social Disorder

Naturally, doing such an anti-social thing as David did would point to an Anti-Social Disorder. As Kim and I looked at what the diagnostic books say about this behavior, I don't personally feel, nor does Kim, that David was a true sociopath. He was of average intelligence even though he thought he had A.D.D., used some unusual methods to manipulate people and, like most all humankind, had some selfishness and impulsiveness. Kim doesn't feel that he had a high degree of unreliability, untruthfulness, unpredictability, or was never sincere in what he did. He did have a high degree of the pleasure principle in him, and for the most part, he got along with the majority of the people with whom he associated. He followed most established rules but this could have been out of fear of punishment because David was always afraid of something. Kim doesn't think David fits this behavior pattern. Of course, the sociopathic personality develops over a lifetime, beginning in early childhood and would not have been as easily detected by Kim as by others since she was with him every day. She had gotten to the point that she often discounted what he said or did by just thinking, "Well, that's just Dave doing his thing."

Borderline Disorder

The Borderline Disorder was considered since self-mutilating acts are a possibility. Of course, suicide would fit that assessment. It is characterized by instability in moods, behavior, self-image, and especially in relationships. As the years went by, Dave became more irritable and temperamental. He would shift from idealizing Kim to a need to devalue her and the children, especially Eric. As Kim has said before, "Dave's self-image interfered with his goal setting. He was not productive in his career. I'm not really sure of Dave's gender identity but there was never a meaningful sexual bond between us. The last few years of our marriage were like a business arrangement."

All the features of Borderline Disorder fit David, especially the moodiness, depression and agitation. Yet based on what Kim told me, I'm more inclined to believe he more clearly fell in the Passive/Aggressive range of characteristics. And based on his actions he would have registered within the severe category.

Manic/Depressive Disorder

There was a possibility that David could have suffered from a Manic/Depressive Disorder. He was never diagnosed with such a disorder and Kim doesn't feel like he had bipolar mood swings. When she first met David she thought for a while that his contagious humor was silly, but as I hear her talk about it, I think it was cyclothymia. This disorder is much less severe than a true bipolar disorder. It can be confused as being a bipolar mood-changing malady. Few people other than his family ever saw how easily David could become frustrated and saw the flashes of anger that he seldom demonstrated in public. Like the other disorders, David did not fit all of the characteristics of cyclothymia.

In the last year or so David was more depressed than elated. To mask his depression he came across as an "everybody's buddy" type person. His family knew better, especially Eric who seemed to catch most of David's wrath.

David Was A.D.D.

After Amy was officially diagnosed with A.D.D., David admitted that as a child he had almost every characteristic that she had. He had had trouble in school as a youngster and had had trouble concentrating on anything long enough to remember it.

It Is For Kim's Benefit

Again, let me engage the reader in reasons why Kim is concerned about the possibility of Dave having suffered from one or more of these disorders. It is not to assess David or diagnose his case. Kim does not wish to highlight his unhealthy childhood or his negative side. It is for her benefit. She needs to know that her children's father was not just a vile man, full of malicious, hateful feelings that somehow grew so demonic that he was satisfying some evil appetite. Kim is convinced that Dave was maladjusted and unable to cope with normal stressors that are a "given" in life.

Kim is aware that the stability of the family affects the children and their children until the unhealthy pattern is broken. She wants to know where that fits her. Is her family pattern broken or can it continue through her? She doesn't want the things she has experienced to ruin her future relationships. She just needs to know what she can change and what she cannot change.

Kim says, "David, I am so full of anger for you — anger that has been there long before you killed the children, but now I'm beginning to understand you, even though it's too late to save you and my children. How I wish I could have know how to help you — to have smoothed your wrinkled thinking like I did your clothes when I pressed them, to have filled your need for revenge like I did your appetite for food. I would have been glad to have cleaned up your messed-up life like I did the mess you always left in the house but you didn't give me a chance. It's so *unfair* for me to have to live without my children, especially because of your personality disorder."

I have convinced Kim that she must not think of David's actions as criminal and label the death of her children as murder. My definition of murder is to take another's life with malicious intent. Considering the accuracy of the pictures Kim has painted of the whole scenario, I am convinced that David's motives, however warped and irrational they were, were not laced with malicious intent to physically harm Kim's children. It was likely that his act was designed to solve a problem that he felt had no other solution.

Kim's response is, "I accept this premise but it's hard to understand why someone would burn down a house to rid it of termites, cut off one's head to cure a toothache, or put out a fire with gasoline. It makes more sense to repair than to destroy, but it's too late to change Dave's faulty thinking and his unacceptable behavior. God only knows why he did what he did and what he thought he was solving. It would make it easier on me if I could see some fairness in it, but I can't."

I had Kim to pray this prayer, "God, please help me to see some sense in this madness. Let this burden I'm having to bear help someone else if it's too late for it to help me. Help me to focus on being a people helper and not be destroyed by selfishness and self-pity. Just help me, Lord. I can't always help myself. When I've done my best, take up the slack with your wonderful grace. But, oh yes, I can see it now. You use people like me to provide the cool water for parched lips, clothes for the naked, companionship for the lonely, and comfort for the bereaved.

I've learned this first hand from the prayers, plane tickets, money, food, and other acts of kindness I received when I was in the pits of grief.

Let me bargain with you, God. Help me to get over this and I'll help others. I'll use this pain I'm going through to make children safer and homes happier. I'll know what 'not' to say to a heartbroken parent who has lost a child, even though I might not know what to say. I'll just say nothing but 'I'm sorry' and be there for them. I'll understand those family members who must survive suicide. You know, Lord, I could be a two-time loser to suicide, or I could be an educated survivor who knows how to help others.

Thanks for making me a free moral agent. I had no choice in my mom's actions when she took her life, or David's action when he took his life and the children's lives. But I do have a choice, though wounded and weary, to help myself by helping others who experience suicide in their family."

With all this information and intensive study, Kim's "gut" feeling is that David had become so "messed up" with prescription drugs that he was paranoid about being arrested and going to jail for buying so many drugs, even though she thinks he always had a legitimate prescription for them. Most people don't go to jail for using prescription drugs. The damage is usually familial and personal.

The incident that Kim related about the night she came home from the Tupperware party was evidence that Dave knew that his "out-of-control" habit was about to come to light and he was severely paranoid about the results. This could be the stressor that pulled the trigger on the pistol that killed Kim's family. She sincerely hopes that anyone with a problem with pain killers will read this and seek help. Though it is embarrassing it can be treated and overcome. Kim pleads with you to let what happened to her family be an impetus for you to get help now.

Kim also hopes this makes those who read this come to respect the doctors more for being cautious about prescribing pain killers or any non-essential medication for prolonged periods of time. Never manipulate your doctor!

One important fact we almost forgot happened the day David killed himself and the children. After the funerals were over, Kim was able to talk with David's boss about his job performance. She learned that on July 17, David's boss had asked him to come in the office later that day to talk about some things. Kim feels like in David's state of mind, he believed he was about to be fired from his job. However, the boss said that that was not the case. He simply wanted to discuss some insurance claims with him.

7

Kim's World Of Grief

When it came time for Kim to begin her closure work in her grief journey, she and I began to write some metaphors and some special feelings she was experiencing at the time. From the beginning of therapy, I had encouraged her to write letters to her children, to David, and to God. These letters make up the next chapter. Much of what you will read in this chapter describes Kim's grief and where she is now in her healing process.

It might seem like a series of independent writings because the articles were all done at different times. Some of them Kim did alone and some are my impressions of how she felt when we were working together. They are all original and relate to Kim's story as she has lived it. Some of it is also information I gave Kim in therapy.

Grief Therapy

Therapy cannot control grief, but it helps the survivor to know when he or she is on target and moving through the healing journey at a healthy pace. If the painful work of grief does not progress properly, it becomes pathological. When this happens, the emotions are so damaged that serious illness, or even death, can occur.

I gave Kim some material which succinctly evaluates all models of grief. This helped her and should be helpful to others.

Some of the feelings Kim experienced were common to anyone who has had a significant loss. She was thinking that "this can't be happening to me! I'll show everybody I'm okay! Don't worry about me; I'm all right. My children are dead but let me help you grieve." These feelings did not harmonize with what had happened, and this reaction was a result of shock because Kim was in the avoidance stage of grief.

When Kim made statements like, "Why did my children leave me? Why can't somebody do something about this pain? Don't say you know how I feel because you've never lost a child," the reactions stemmed from emotions of anger and rage.

She reached another stage when she said, "My children are gone." At this point grief work began in earnest. All of the pain and stress was healthy and normal in dealing with her grief.

If this depression had persisted for a prolonged period of time, and she had not had professional help, Kim would have been in trouble.

Finally, there was a sense of permanency. The pain was not going away. A resurrection was taking place. At this point Kim began to try to make the best of it. Coping mechanisms began to kick in. She decided that the problem was not going away and she began to work it out the best way possible. This was acceptance.

Kim re-experienced all these feelings as the healing process continued. Each day a new limitation became real and acceptance was accomplished by mini-grief processes. She got "bogged down" in this stage a few times and needed some help or a "jump start" to get the grief process up and running again. When one gets bogged down in grief, he or she should not hesitate to ask doctors, nurses, ministers, social workers, or just a friend to help him or her find someone who specializes in grief recovery. Funeral homes, churches and service organizations have seminars or provide counselors to help with the coping techniques needed for good grief. Caregivers are eager to help and are usually well trained but unless mourners care enough to get help, it probably will never be effective. The best stage of grief is when the griever takes personal responsibility to get over the loss even if it means asking for help.

It is virtually impossible to find a grief model that fits every person who will ever grieve. Even the experts use different terms for different stages. Grief recovery counselors are faced with broad, and sometimes, unpredictable stages of emotions. It is not unusual for parents who have lost children to shift in and out of these emotions for months and years.

It becomes pathological when the parent gets locked into a non-acceptance set of emotions such as denial, numbness, disbelief or volatile emotions such as anger and hostility. Sometimes a prolonged yearning or sense of being undone, disorganized, or preoccupied with the deceased, becomes chronic depression, helplessness and loneliness.

Good emotions lead to acceptance, resolution, re-establishment, relief, reintegration, reinvestment, reorganization and cognition or understanding of one's personal responsibility to get over the death.

As time goes on, you really get the feeling of wanting to be a part of life again and that's when closure can take place.

Cultures that allow outward, public display of emotions have fewer cases of morbid grief than those with restricted emotions. Imploded emotions eventually explode in some way, somewhere, somehow.

Mourners who have developed brittle emotions over a long maturation period cannot expect to suddenly experience healthy, stable emotions when a child has died. I often refer to a person's "baggage wagon" (passed negative experiences) when discussing how people grieve and how the past affects their present. This is why Kim and I wrote the chapter on *Family Dynamics* that dealt with her family history.

The Looking Glass

Kim described her experience like this: Like Alice in Wonderland, I now often go through the looking glass into the fantasy world of my past life. It is a world of memories and fading images — a world far from perfect yet one that I miss. I miss the laughter, the tears, the tension and the mundaneness of life with my family. It was a world that was concrete and sensate with no room to guess what was coming next. I knew the rules; what was expected. I thought my world had definite boundaries with clear cut responsibilities but it didn't. Now my world is a bit less clear, less secure, and a lot more empty.

Emptiness

It is the emptiness I loathe the most; a world void of the voices of my children, no phone calls from them, no bursting through the door at 4:00 P.M., filling the air with talk of the day. It is a quiet world where there are no shoulders to hug or cheeks to kiss, no heads of hair for me to run my fingers through. There are no phones ringing, no school books, no papers, no projects or assignments to do, no teenagers in and out of my house. My house is quiet and orderly but very empty.

I guess I should be thankful I had those days and those times, but gratitude is swallowed up by grief and loss. The hardest thing is to come to the realization there is nothing I can do to change this. It was a terminal choice that I did not make, and yet I must live with it every minute.

Land Mines

There are many land mines waiting for me in my journey through life now. They are larger, more powerful and more covert than they have ever been. Each one holds its own particular danger and form of destruction. I am left to navigate for the next 40-50 years of life through this maze without being destroyed or destroying others.

My path is filled with "booby traps" called rage, anger, hostility, unforgiveness, resentfulness, retaliation, and self-pity. Those are the obvious ones. Less obvious, yet more subtle and just as deadly are the enemies of cynicism, withdrawal, and despair. Loss of hope and faith are also peppered in my path life. Selfishness is buried along the periphery of these mines. When I become selfish, I know I am on unstable ground. The most dangerous aspect of the mines along the path is that they are always directly under a mirage or an oasis. This oasis promises comfort, justice and restitution from my pain, but these mirages are meant to lure the unsuspecting grieving widow to the brink of shelter and refreshment only to destroy. And so I must navigate through this maze to reach my destination.

A Barren Wilderness

Sometimes I feel like I'm in a barren wilderness all alone. The loneliness had a permanence and weight all its own. It became heavier and heavier as the sun went down, reaching its peaks at dusk and at bedtime. It was often smothering, crushing and paralyzing. The loneliness sapped my energy and desire. It even attacks me now when I am not alone. Sometimes it even attacks me when I am with my closest friends. Loneliness is ruthless — it's a deadly barren wilderness.

An Earthquake

I helped Kim write this metaphor that I felt described her grief journey. My grief for the most part has been like an earthquake. Even though on the surface life goes on like business as usual, below the surface unsettled forces are stirring, always ready to burst into a furious convulsion. When my inner feelings finally come out, I feel helpless, useless, and unworthy to live. My whole world succumbs to the forces of grief, like the earth must submit to the authority of an earthquake. I feel like I am losing my mind or even dying.

Aftershock

Again, Kim described her feelings when she said that I was suddenly, without my permission, thrust on the battlefield of life. My way of life had been demolished. All I could see were smoldering ruins of a life that I had lived. Rubble was everywhere. Now I was left to sift through smoke and ashes to see what was left, but I was wounded — almost mortally. I was dazed, confused, bleeding and in pain. I coughed at the smoke. My eyes and nostrils burned with the smell of smoke and death. My emotions were paralyzed, yet I was filled with rage. I had no strength to fight back. All I could do was to sit in the ash heap and cry. And that's what I did. I cried almost non-stop for days.

Then there was "The Choice". The decision was easy to make, but hard to keep. Did I want to survive and overcome, or did I want to die, too? There were no other choices. There was no middle ground. I was to overcome or be destroyed. Which would it be? As badly as I wanted to die along with my children, my rage became the impetus that kept me going. I was furious and had anger-spurred energy that I had never felt before. I said to the enemy, "So help me God, I will not let you take me down, too. You will not defeat me."

I used my anger for strength to survive. It would take every bit of strength I could muster to do the things I would need to do from that point. Daily survival became the most difficult thing I had ever had to face.

After two funerals came the cleanup — tasks that must be done. These tasks were the puzzle pieces in the jigsaw of survival that I had never before encountered and wasn't quite sure what to do. I, and I alone, had to make many life-changing decisions in a very short period of time. Where was I to live now? What would I do with their things? What about a job? Never before had I had only one person to consider — me. It was frightening and very lonely. I was unencumbered, free and totally miserable.

Labor Pains

As I began to write this book, nine months after my day of tragedy, I felt that I had escaped the ravages of morbid grief even though I knew that my "labor pains", much like those felt when giving birth to my babies, were not yet over, though nine months were up.

Waves Of Grief

I helped Kim with this metaphor, referring to her vacation at the beach. Since I had just enjoyed a wonderful, peaceful vacation at the beach with my family, and had observed the beautiful waves as they came crashing toward the shore, I'd like to use the waves to describe how my grief works. It's like I have just been out in the ocean, jumping the waves, floating up above the danger of the world, admiring the vastness of the sea which seems to have no beginning. I was awe struck by the colorful hue of the water as the sun bounced off its surface, which caused me to be unaware of the dangers around me. Then I lost concentration, looked away instantaneously from the waves, and with a sudden and powerful force they rolled over me and swallowed me up and rendered me helpless for what seemed like forever.

When I finally regained my footing by the aid of those around me, I started plowing through the water as quickly as I could toward the safety of the shore and then — unexpectedly another wave came and took me under again. I was strangled by the salty water. It took my breath. It burned my eyes. It frightened me and I was sure I was going to drown. Somehow I regained my footing and, as quickly as possible, pushed toward the shore. When I thought I was almost there, another wave came but thankfully the closer I got to the shore, the less powerful the waves were and my recovery time was not quite as long.

My grief comes in waves, little waves, medium-size waves, and sometimes, large thundering waves. I'm almost to the shore. I can almost feel the warm, smooth sand under my feet.

I'm almost there, Amy. Mama's going to be all right. Eric, you don't have to help Mama up now, I'm almost there. I'll be okay. Your unending love for me will always be the wave that lifts me and keeps me above the danger of depression and failure. I'm almost there. Just a few little waves are breaking at my feet now. I'm winning the battle against the powerful waves of grief.

I Don't Want To Drown

It's ironic that as I was helping Kim with the metaphor on the waves, she was writing this not knowing what I was doing. Grief comes thundering over me like an ocean wave pounding me into the current of emotions, leaving me dazed, confused, pulling me under, making me struggle to survive. I feel like I am drowning. Sometimes I want to drown. I am helpless and very tired. Who will save me from this? Who will rescue my soul from its clutches? Many pass by in their seafaring vessels. Some pass by out of apathy and do not notice my plight. Some pass by out of curiosity and gaze and wave as I struggle for life. Some circle around me and shout, "I don't know what to say." They seem to want to help but don't know how. Some pass by and say, "I'm sorry but you must get yourself out of your sea of grief." A few venture close enough to feel my pain and touch my grief. They are the faithful friends for whom I am ever grateful. They don't mind if they get wet, or get water up their noses, too, or gasp for breath trying to help me. They often let me aboard their ships for a while so I can catch my breath. But grief must, and does, pull me back again into the current and I must fight this fight alone once more. On the one hand, I want to drown; on the other, I yearn to live.

An Amputation

It was an amputation, not of limbs or appendages, but of the heart. It was as if my body and soul were placed on a gigantic paper cutter and then clamped shut like a guillotine. In an instant, my heart was severed from my body, leaving me empty inside, never to be the same again. Somehow I must learn to live without my heart. How am I to do this? How am I to live my life with vital pieces of myself missing? My children, of course, were not me, but they were essential to my life. When I was a child I often thought about the children I would have. I wanted desperately to have many children, even when I was just a child myself. All my hopes and dreams focused on Eric and Amy and I loved them more than I can describe. When they died, a portion of my own soul died, too, and my own identity was damaged. My heart was cut out.

Fading Memories

I loved being a mother. From the time I knew I was pregnant, I was so excited. My children were very much planned and wanted. The pain of childbirth seemed to pale in comparison to the joy of creating a new life. I look back and cherish all the moments I had with them. Even the diapers, the spitting up, the fevers, the earaches, and the colic now seem so special. How was I to know that these times would soon pass and become only fading memories? How can one capture time?

Having To Grieve Alone

The loneliness and the dread I had of coming home to a deathly quiet house and having to grieve alone were so scary. Sometimes I thought I was going crazy or I might even be dying and the loneliness exacerbated those feelings. I cried every day when I came home. I wasn't just tearing up, I was weeping and wailing and sobbing until I was nauseated. Sometimes my heart was physically affected by the emotional stress caused by my grief. I could not see my therapist every day and I couldn't ask my friends to be there when I got home every day to help me. I had to do it alone but I needed someone to love me and say I was okay. I needed a warm body to hold me and take some of the fear away. If I died I wanted someone there to comfort me. I didn't want to die alone. On numerous occasions I would lose control and end up wailing for my children but there was no one there but the four walls. I moaned and groaned like a wounded animal. I made sounds that I had never heard before. I can't even repeat some of them. No one was there to help me up when I fell prostrate on my face. I literally could not stand up. My legs would not hold me up but there was no one there on which to lean.

I Haven't Grieved For David

The only person I haven't grieved for is David. I've been so angry with him that I've delayed grieving his death. Little by little I am beginning to miss some of the things he did or said. I miss his temperament. During the first part of our marriage, he was very easygoing, very laid back on the outside but now I know that on the inside, he was seething, which is odd, but I miss the temperament I perceived. There are other little idiosyncrasies about him that I miss, like some inside jokes between us. Our whole family had some little jokes among ourselves. I'm the only one left who knows about them and I miss having David around to share them with me.

Holding On To Grief

I helped Kim with this closure thought. Giving up my grief means that my two precious children will only live as historical beings. I want them to live so badly that I struggle emotionally as the natural body often struggles to maintain life when mortally wounded. I don't enjoy this exhausting struggle, but it seems almost like an obsession to me. My episodes of grief are the only way I know to keep me connected with, and hold on to, Amy and Eric.

My Dreams

I'm going to let Kim talk about her dreams, and when appropriate I will offer my interpretations. I want to talk about some of the dreams I've had after the death of my family and what they mean to me, especially as they relate to my grief.

The most recent dream I had is kinda fuzzy so I don't remember all of the details, but it took place in a candy store. There was candy all over the four walls. The whole dream was almost like a mystery novel. Someone had killed my children and it had something to do with the Mafia. It was a cover-up and I was trying to figure out who the killer was by trying to lure him back to the scene. I was going to get set up in the store in such a way that he would want to come back and we would know who he was. I don't remember Dave being in this dream but the kids were there and they were dead, if that makes any sense.

I recall part of another dream where someone was trying to shoot me in the back of the head. The painful thing about this dream was that I was trying so hard to figure out what it would be like to be shot.

A lot of my dreams have to do with me being shot and I think it has to do with my need to know what it was like for the kids when they died. Did it hurt? Were they scared? Maybe part of it is that I don't feel that it was right for them to die and me to live. They died and I was the one that deserved it and should have died instead of them. That makes me feel sad and frustrated and maybe that is why I dream these dreams over and over about David or someone else coming after me with a gun.

I've dreamed about David several times. In one particular dream, I dreamed that he had already killed the children and himself but he came back to the house and I was confronting him about it, saying, "How could you have done this?" Every time I would turn my back on him, he had a gun and I would take it away from him, turn my back again, and he would have another one. He had a smirk on his face and he said, "I'm really after you", and one time I said, "Okay, David, I know you're going to kill me, so go ahead and get it over with — just do it." Then he pointed the gun at the back of my head and I could literally feel the bullet going in. It was a really scary dream and when I woke up, I was shaking and crying and physically exhausted.

As Kim's therapist I interpreted this dream to be connected with the fact that she believes, even though it is purely speculation, that if she had been there when the homicide/suicide was taking place, that David would have killed her, too. It could mean that she feels that when he killed the children, he killed her by proxy, which creates an unusual need for her to know how they felt when they died. Of course, she has some ambivalence about that because on the one hand, she would have wanted to die with all of them, and on the other hand, she has natural survival instincts and resist death. The thought of death is scary.

Another time, soon after this, I dreamed about him again and I vigorously asked him, "Dave, why did you do this? Just why did you do it?" He had the weirdest, most bizarre look on his face. His eyes had this real evil look and he just laughed, and laughed and laughed like he was getting the last laugh; like I've done this to you and I'm glad. That was a horrible dream and causes me mental anguish.

I feel like this dream deals with Kim's strong feelings that David killed her children to punish her for putting them before him, or that he felt like she was unfaithful to him. It was probably the last episode of the constant covert power struggle that went on in their marriage. For the most part, it had evolved that the children believed that Kim was the strong one in their family. In Dave's mind, Kim had the upper hand in the "mental arm wrestling" that goes on in interpersonal relationships. Knowing this, while Kim is asleep, her mind replays the power struggle and now Dave has won. He got in the last blow and it was a fatal one.

I want to dream about Amy. I've had one peaceful dream about Eric but I can't seem to have the same kind of dream about Amy which I believe would ease my mind about her welfare.

I feel like a lot of this was probably fostered by some things that have come up in therapy or maybe some things that Kim has read about closure coming when you have a peaceful dream about the loved one who has died.

I Want Them To Come Back

Part of me feels a little angry with God because He won't let them come back in spirit. I know that sounds crazy, but you read so much about people seeing the ghost of their loved ones and I wonder why I haven't had such an experience. I know if the kids could come back as a ghost or anything else, they would, knowing how much I need to see them. My Bible understanding is that there's a great gulf between the living and the dead, and neither can pass from one place to the other. I guess that's true because I know my kids would try to reach me if they could. The burning desire for my kids to contact me one more time makes me want to dream about them or see a ghost of them, even though it probably would scare me out of my wits. I don't understand all about ghosts and spirits, but for me the bottom line is, I'd like to have a peaceful dream about Amy and feel like she's okay.

In one of the last dreams I've had, the kids were saying that heaven wasn't all that it was "cracked up" to be. I was asking them if they had seen God and they said, "Oh, yes, we see Him every day", like it was no big deal to them at all. They said, "You know, we still have to work and have things to do", like it wasn't that different from being home. It was typical teenage talk.

I'm disappointed because I would have wanted them to say, "Heaven is wonderful and we're having a great time", or something like that. I must feel in competition with God since He's got my children and I want them back even though I know they are His.

Is Dave In Heaven?

A part of me thinks, "Why are they up there having a good time and I'm not?" When I think about being in heaven I think that if Dave went to heaven, wouldn't that be rewarding him? It seems like he got what he wanted. He took everybody to heaven and they're up there having a good time and I'm here having to struggle with all the fallout. That makes me mad. I'm just really ticked off because I feel like he should have to pay somehow. He ought to burn in Hell. I don't want him to burn for a long time but just for a few minutes, just long enough for me to say, "Okay, you've paid your dues." I know that Jesus is the Savior and Judge and He's paid for everything but for some reason (maybe that power struggle thing), I just don't want Dave to be let off the hook. It seems like all of his life he just sort of got off the hook.

I pray that God will help me to forgive him and that I can put this in its place without feeling so angry. It's going to take a long time but I'm trying. I'm working through it.

The children are with Jesus and that is my one consolation. They were innocent. I knew each of their hearts as well as any mortal could have and truly feel that they are in heaven with God. In their adolescent way they were trying to do what was right.

Pain In The Back

When the most intense seizures of grief came upon Kim, she began to experience some of the most debilitating back pain she had ever known. It was hard for her to believe that grief could cause such physical pain and soreness in certain areas of her body. She would be on the floor for up to two hours before she could get up. At times she could not get herself in a position to get out of bed. Not one soul was there to help her nor to give her security. She was not sure for a while that I knew what I was talking about when I said it was connected with her grief. I told her she was experiencing somatization. Being vaguely familiar with the term through her medical training as a Med Tech and her counseling studies at Troy State, Kim was not frightened by the term at all. Having an inquisitive mind she asked, "What is your definition of somatization?"

I first told her about Tammy Starling, a young widow whose husband, Dr. Milton Startling, was accidentally killed when he was returning to his office during a winter freeze in Charlotte, North Carolina. Tammy was expecting a child within two months and she delayed her grief work until about six months later. She began to experience lower back pain which I thought I recognized as a physical manifestation of intense grief.

I went on to define somatization as physical symptoms of unacceptable, unconscious feelings. These feelings are picked up by the autonomic nervous system and are transferred to the body cells. The word *soma* in the Greek means "body cell".

True to my prediction, Kim's "pain in the back" subsided when she began to deal with her grief in an open, realistic way. When she looks back over the history of her back pain, she can see that it usually affected her when she was under stress. Even when she thought that she had injured her back, it had come when her stress level was abnormally high. This seems to indicate that she's experienced somatization to some degree for a good portion of her adult life.

I realize that many widows or widowers identify with the things I've mentioned about Kim. Untold thousands of grievers have emotional somatization and I hope therapists will be trained to help their clients understand it when it's connected with emotional pain.

8 Letters

Communication is considered by some therapists to be the best way to resolve conflict. If the person suffering as a result of the conflict can't physically speak with the others involved, they are often asked to write letters to the persons with whom he or she wishes to communicate.

This is why Kim has written these letters to God, David and her children. I had hoped she would write a letter to her mother but she seemed to find ways to avoid such a letter.

These are her letters.

A Letter to God

Dear God,

Where were you on July 17, 1995? Were you in heaven looking down as all the wheels began to turn on the sequence of events that day? I know in your omniscience you knew what would happen next. Are you really aware of all things at all times, or were you preoccupied with other matters of the universe? Was your mind on Bill Clinton, Bosnia, or starving children in Asia? I know the Bible says, "Your ways are higher than our ways and your thoughts higher than ours." I know you also wondered if Job would condemn you when bad things happened to him. I know those things in my head, but my heart asks, Where were you? So, please don't strike me dead while I'm working through this. There are some things I just have to ask you.

If you knew this would happen to me, why did you allow me to be born in the first place? Or, David for that matter? Why in the course of events did you not warn me as to what type of person he might become? Why do you keep the future such a secret? If you had only warned me, I could have escaped with the kids. But I chose to stay with Dave mostly out of wanting to be obedient to your laws concerning marriage.

You have said, "The way of the transgressor is hard." Well, so is the way of the obedient.

When the children died, I was just not sure I wanted to be obedient anymore. It certainly seemed only to complicate my life and not to help. The price I had to pay was just too costly.

But, you in your divine patience are helping me to deal with how I feel about you. Your enduring love has prevented you from opening up Hell and swallowing me up for such thoughts. But I still can't help but wonder. Why did you make things this way? And, why did you not intervene? Is there some great cosmic plan in all of this, or is it just a "crap shoot"? Or, somewhere in between?

What good is prayer if we are not "delivered from evil"? But when I think of these things I am reminded that your Son was also mistreated and murdered. You allowed your Son and yourself incarnate to experience pain, loss, rejection and disappointment. Why? If you are God, why did you allow this? It makes no sense to me.

Why did you allow Jesus to die on the cross? Why did it have to be this way? When Jesus was asking, "My God, My God, Why have you forsaken me?" You were saying, "My Son, My Son, What have they done to you?"

Why did it have to be this way?

Another Letter to God

Dear God,

From the time I was a little girl, I remember being curious about you. I wondered who you were and longed to hear stories about you. I got most of my information from my next door neighbor who was also six. My parents rarely mentioned you except in vain. My mother, however, did tell me you lived in heaven and that it was a good place and if I were good I could go there, and if I were bad I would go to the bad place where bad people went. Since I didn't want to go there, I determined to be good so that I could go to heaven. Also, I remember one time sitting on my front steps as a child and looking into the clouds hoping to see you. I was sure I caught a glimpse of you so I ran and told my mother than I had seen God. She didn't believe me but I was convinced anyway. Throughout my young life I wanted to know more about you. My parents didn't go to church but I resolved that when I could drive I would go every Sunday. I wanted to know how to be good enough to go to heaven.

As I grew and read the Bible more I fell in love with you more and more. You seemed to bless my life also. You gave me a husband and two beautiful children.

You were there for me when my mother died and when daddy got in trouble. You were there when no one else was during the loneliness of my younger years. I loved you and leaned on you.

Then you gave me happiness in a career and in a family. You made my life complete with the children you gave me.

I always knew they were yours and that you had only loaned them to me.

I remember once when Eric was a baby and had been sick, I was talking with my friend, Jane, whose baby had had open heart surgery. I remarked that I didn't know how she could handle that and I didn't know what I would do if that ever happened to Eric. I will always remember what she said and the wisdom of her words are now timeless to me. She said, "Kim, our children are not promised to us. They belong to God and He allows us to keep them as long as He wants. I know if my little girl died she would go straight to the arms of Jesus. So I'm not afraid if she dies."

Jane never knew how much that conversation affected me. I have reflected on it time and time again over the years. But when the children died, I was so angry with you, God, for taking my children away!

I felt betrayed by my best friend. I know you didn't pull the trigger but you didn't intervene. That is why I'm angry with you. You were supposed to be Protector and Defender and you didn't even intervene. Are you really who you say you are?

Letters to My Children

10/31/95

My dearest Eric,

My firstborn of my heart and soul. Though you are gone from me, you live in my heart forever. You will always be a joy to my heart. You will be the music of violins to my grieving soul. You will be as the gentle breeze of the spring morning. You will be the soft rain that falls in the evening. You will always remind me of the joys of life — the joy of being a mother.

Today I remember your birthday. On that beautiful Monday, November 5th, when I knew that that would be "the day", it was as if I wanted to memorize every portion of it. I wanted to commit to memory all the sights and sounds of that day so they would be etched on my heart forever, and they are. The morning was crisp and cool — perfect weather, perfectly blue skies with a kind of white clouds — a new day, a new beginning, a new life for you and me.

The moment you were delivered the doctor told me you were a boy. What a strange and awesome feeling! How could a boy come from my body? How could my body produce a living being? What an awesome God we serve.

When he delivered you, you were crying. He placed your purple little body on my stomach and I stroked you and called your name. It was as if you knew my voice already and began to stop crying. That moment sealed us and bonded us forever. From that moment 'till eternity, I was and will be hopelessly enthralled by you, my son, loving you with every fiber of my being.

2/13/96

Dear Amy,

How I have missed you, my precious darling daughter. Though grief is sometimes unbearable, I know you are in the Master's arms. I wonder if it has been a good day for you, if all your days are filled with goodness. I hope so, for you, my precious love of my life. Today seemed like a Spring day, and as usual, I thought of you, my cherished child. This morning while I cooked grits, I thought of how you loved them, and how you called them "grips" and always had them in your hair.

I know it will soon be your birthday. You would have been fourteen. I think of your laughter — your wonderful sense of humor. I miss that, and you, my precious child. How can I go on without you?

I wish you were here to know Charles. He keeps me going through my despair over you and Eric. He is warm and loving. I wonder how the three of you would get along. It is a hard transition for me, Amy, to leave the thoughts of you and have a new family again. I got a letter from one of your best friends from Virginia. I miss the days when you and she would be playing together. I miss all of the days I had with you and Eric.

How could your daddy have taken you from me? How can I face another summer without you two? How can I go to the beach and not find you there? How can I live with the fact that I will not see you again this side of heaven? I am consoled in the fact that Christ is there and you are with Him. I hope He will make something come of this pain.

3/13/96

Dear Eric & Amy,

Today is a beautiful Spring day. The sun is shining. The birds are singing. There is a soft breeze blowing here on earth. It would have been a day that you two would have enjoyed. I can see you now, Amy, walking Shiloh up to our neighbor's house. She misses you, you know, and has moved to Florida. Eric, I can see you throwing the ball, or practicing guitar right now. I wonder if you are playing instruments in heaven. I hope the weather there is perfect all the time. I hope you feel happy and fulfilled. Dr. Gunnells told me that you would probably be telling me to let you go. I want to, but it is so hard. Letting you go would mean to send you off into eternity without me. Well, that is where you are already. Would letting you go mean forgetting all the wonderful things about you two? How can I bury your memories like I buried your bodies? What can I do to make the memory of you linger — your smiles, your voices, your touches, your laughter? How can I let go of these forever?

Amy, were you frightened when you had to die? Did you see Jesus right away and did He make you feel calm and safe?

What was it like for you, Eric? Were you afraid? Did Jesus calm you as well? I hope He gave you a special grace to endure what you had to go through. I am confident He did.

Eric, I loved you so much as well. You were my Rock. I leaned on you a lot and you probably didn't even know it. You were strong and talented and had such a good heart. I was proud of you and I admired you. I remember a few days before you died, on one of those rare instances when you came to me for affection, you came and sat on the couch with me, and I ran my fingers through the back of your hair and held your hand. I will always remember the special closeness of those moments. I remember how you looked — those beautiful brown eyes and that beautiful smile. You were so handsome! I loved you so much and I miss you from the depths of my inner being.

You came to me the other night in my dreams. We hugged for a long time and we seemed to communicate a mutual love that was so strong! I remember wondering if it was the real you and feeling of your face and knowing it was you. I remember us talking for a long time and I asked you if you knew that you had died. Who killed you? Then when I asked if you were real, you vanished! Eric, it was almost more than I could bear to give you up again.

Eric and Amy, working through this grief and loss of you is so hard. Sometimes it feels as if my chest has been cut open and all of my insides have been pulled out and there is a big gaping hole in my heart.

Most of the time I feel numb. I wonder if I'll ever recover from this. I wonder what to do with myself and the rest of my life. I hope God will find a way to redeem all of this.

Eric and Amy, if I could reach back in time and hold you to my breast, then maybe my soul would be at rest. If I could touch you one last time — to feel you near — to see your smile — to hear your voice — but, someone took you — and you were mine.

3/14/96

Dear Amy,

Life seems so empty without you. I went shopping today. Oh, how I miss the times we had when we would go shopping! I remember getting your ears pierced the Monday before you died. The pain was so excruciating when the police gave me your earrings back. They were supposed to be in your ears and your ears were supposed to be around until you had grown old.

What am I to do with myself now that you're gone? Who can I ever love like I loved you? You were everything to me. I have never loved another human being as much as I loved you. I wanted you and thought about you since I was a little girl. I imagined the day when I would have a daughter of my own. How was I to know that you, my love, would have been so special? You were so beautiful from the day you were born. When you were born, I felt so complete. I loved nursing you in the swing in the back yard on beautiful Spring days. I loved feeling you taking nourishment from by body. As you grew, you became more and more beautiful.

When you went to school you had such a hard time. I wanted to rescue you from everything and everyone that caused you pain. I wanted to fight all your battles for you. It hurt me so much to see you cry.

I loved rubbing your back and touching your "stubby fingers". I loved singing to you at night before you went to bed. Our favorite was "I'll Fly Away". My dear, you have already flown away. Why could I not go with you? We also loved, "Bye,

Bye, Lu Lay". Remember we also liked that song that I would sing to you when you were upset, which started off, "Rest, the Lord is near."

4/8/96

Dear Amy,

Today is the day before your 14th birthday. I'm at the Shakespeare Festival. It is one of those few places on earth that reminds me of heaven. It is peaceful here. You would enjoy the ducks and the swans today. When I see the brick building, it reminds me of the mansions that might be in heaven. I wonder if yours looks like this. I'm sure yours is so much better. I hope that God allows mine to be there next to yours. I'm sure He will allow it when I get there.

Amy, I'm buying you and Eric and Dave a tombstone tomorrow. I've been putting it off — it seems too final. But Charles says you need one so I'll take care of it on your birthday. I'm bringing you some flowers tomorrow, too. I hope in some way you can look down and see them. I love you.

6/16/96

My dearest Eric,

I have thought of you so much lately. I talked to one of your friends today. She still has the picture you drew on her memo board. She's taking it with her to Oklahoma.

I still remember a vivid picture of you in my mind. I remember you holding that little boy under your arm and running with him across the playground. You were so good with those boys. I couldn't wait to see what you would be like as a father.

Maybe in heaven, my dearest Son, all your dreams will be fulfilled. You and I always loved Star Wars and Star Trek. I hope you are navigating across the universe to unknown worlds. I hope you can play music effortlessly like the Masters. I hope you can converse with all of the greats of the past. I remember when you were about two years old you asked me, "Mommy, are there little chairs in heaven?" Eric, you used to ask me to draw God. Now I'm asking you to draw Him. You know firsthand what He looks like and sounds like.

I was in the Mall yesterday and I wondered how differently you might feel about life on earth now that you have tasted eternity. You used to be so conscious of style in clothes and shoes and even wanted those $100 Oakleys. I wonder now how you would feel about those things. I wonder what wisdom and insight you would share with me after living in Paradise.

My precious son, how I wish I could just talk with you on the phone. I miss your voice! I miss your smile! I remember the scar on your cheek from where you fell on a toy train as a toddler. It seems unreal that I will never see that scar on your cheek again.

I remember touching your hand in the casket. I expected it to be warm but it was cold. It sent a cold chill like a knife penetrating my heart to know that you were really dead. How could one I loved so much be gone forever, without my permission, without my opinion, or say so? If I could only have been able to negotiate with God, or with David. "My life for Eric's," I would gladly say. I loved you so much, my son, my darling. Nothing can ever compare to what I feel for you.

I remember you used to sing a song that said, "Hold on for one more day." I repeat it over and over as if you are telling me to hold on. It is hard but I'm holding on for you and me.

7/25/96

To Eric,

I loved you so much and I thank God for allowing me to be your mom for a little while. I enjoyed you and you taught me so much about life and love. I appreciate you for the son you were to me and the person you were. You were handsome, talented and responsible. You loved the Lord and you loved your family. You loved me.

But most important, Eric, is that you gave me a glimpse of what it was like for God to see His Son murdered. The magnitude of salvation is now so apparent. The hope of a resurrection is so real when I look at your grave. But more than anything, I want to deliver a crushing blow to Satan for what he did to you by overcoming evil with good.

Good-bye, my son. I love you eternally. Thank you for everything.

Mom

Final Letter to Amy

7/25/96

Dear Amy,

I thank God for letting me be your mom for a little while. You were the light of my life and you taught me so much about love and acceptance. I have rescued you from every pain in your life except from the one you loved and trusted. I wish I had been there for you when you needed me most. I wish I had died in your place.

So help me, Amy, I will do everything in my power to honor yours and Eric's memory by overcoming evil with good.

Good-bye, my Amy. I loved you with my whole life.

Mom

Letter to David

Dear David,

It's been one year and one month and I'm only now beginning to grieve for you. I suppose it's taken this long for the shock to wear off and this long for me to wade through the rubble of grief for the children and finally make my way to grieve for you. And I do.

I really did love you, you know. Or, maybe you didn't know it. Maybe you were unaware of my love. Maybe I was harsh with you or sarcastic and it cut you deeper than I ever knew. I'm so sorry.

Only now do I wish I could have been there for you. To hold you and rock you and kiss away your troubles. If only I had known your pain was so deep.

If only. If only.

I suppose if all the "if onlys" were stacked together end to end like bricks, I could walk on them from here to eternity.

If only I had known how bad you were hurting.

If only I knew how to save you from drowning.

If only I had known how to fix you.

If only I had known how to make you feel better.

If only I had loved you more.

Done more.

Been more.

Maybe you would have not made this choice.

If only I could have read your troubled mind that day.

If only there had been some soothing ointment for your

broken heart.

If only I had not let you kept that gun in the house.

If only I could have reasoned with you.

If only I could have looked beyond myself to see your troubled mind.

If I had only known what to do I would have done it . . .

A million times!

But I didn't.

And you did what you did without my permission — or God's.

Why, David, Why?

Did you make this bad choice because you were sick . . .

Or, were you sick because you made a series of bad choices?

You were sick and I couldn't heal you.

You were broken and I couldn't fix you.

You were drowning and I couldn't save you.

I guess I'm not God (I almost forgot that).

But even God allowed you to make your own choice.

He was there for you —

He threw out the life saver but you didn't get it.

You didn't cling to it when the storm was raging.

The waves swept over you and you let go!

Why did you let go, David?

Why did you have no strength left to hang on?

God is the source of our strength —

Why were you empty?

Were you empty because you did not go to the well?

I know the well is not dry!

Or, was it like driving through the desert on half a tank of
gas -

Did you just run out of gas?

Or, is it like the parable of the Ten Virgins —

Did you just not get enough oil at the store?

Oh, my precious husband —

It was so hard for me to see you self-destruct.

David, I watched you die little by little all through the
years.

Little by little.

Drop by drop.

Like an eroding landscape.

It was so subtle — so slow that when you finally imploded,

I was so surprised.

I didn't see it coming.

Or, did I, but looked the other way?

God, forgive me.

David, forgive me.

I didn't know what to do!

9

A Widow And Childless Mother

In this chapter I asked Kim to describe her life after the death of her family. Among some of the first statements she made were: "One minute I was married, the next minute I was a widow. I had two children and in an instant they were gone."

Kim's Life Now

This was the first time since college that I had been alone and had absolutely no one to consider but myself. When I was alone in college, it was okay and it felt good to be independent. But that was before I became a wife and mother.

After I got married and had kids, I had enmeshed my life into theirs. When I lost them, I felt an emptiness that I had never felt before. I was angry, hurt and very afraid. Not only did I feel alone but I felt the awful sense of being abandoned by my husband and children. This was probably worsened by my separation anxiety stemming from the death of my mother almost thirty years ago.

There were some weird dynamics that came with grief and being left all alone. I couldn't understand how I could feel a sense of relief. This relief was not something I wanted but a cloud of reality fell upon me. I was alone and responsible for no one but me. All the responsibilities with which I had been encumbered were gone and I didn't know how to act with the new freedom. I would have gladly traded it to have my family back.

I didn't know what to do with myself. It had been so long since I had a free lifestyle I didn't know what to do with my time when I was not working or how to spend my money. Everyone needs to be accountable to someone but I didn't have anyone, not one person to whom I was accountable.

One weekend I decided to go to Florida. I started feeling funny and I thought, "I need to call someone to let them know where I'm going." Then it dawned on me that there was no one to call. I was an adult. I didn't have to get permission or even let anyone know where I was. That was a very strange feeling, having no one to make any demands on me or to expect anything of me. The feeling soon turned to sadness because with all of this new freedom there was no one to care about me. There was no one in my inner circle but me. My friends and family cared but they had their own lives and they weren't used to my new lifestyle either. So it was just me — "24 x 7" which adds up to all the time.

I was talking with a friend about purchasing something that was going to be expensive so I said, "Well, it doesn't really matter because I don't have anyone to spend any money on." She looked so hurt because she felt bad for me, yet I wasn't saying it for pity. It was just the way I felt. Money didn't have the same meaning anymore. I could care less whether I had one dime or a million dollars. Money was not important except for paying the regular monthly bills.

It didn't make any difference whether I worked or not. What more can I say? It was such an incredible, disoriented feeling, just a feeling of — Who cares? What difference does it make?

One good thing that has come out of this tragedy is that I don't let material things bother me like they used to. I've already experienced the ultimate loss and when you've already lost the most important thing in your life, there is nothing left to lose. There isn't anything left on this earth worth worrying your brains out over. Be it good or bad, that's the attitude I had from being freed from my responsibility as a wife and mother.

As a childless mother, I miss the passion I had when the children were alive. They caused me to want to work so things could be good for them and I spent most of my money on them. I now had to say good-bye to motherhood.

A Monologue To Eric And Amy

Eric and Amy, I miss you, not only for who you were, but for who I was when I was with you. I miss the mother I was when I rocked you to sleep as infants. I miss the feeling of your baby soft skin and hair against my cheek. I miss the feeling and smell of your hot little milk breath upon my face.

As you grew, I miss the mom/nurse I was when I doctored your skinned knees and gave you medicine when you were feverish. I miss the mom/comforter I was when I held you as you cried when you were hurt or disappointed. I miss crying with you when I felt you were wronged.

I miss the sound of my voice singing songs to you. I miss my prayers that went up with yours as we prayed together about things in each of your lives.

I miss the mom/instructor I was as I tried to teach you about life and about God. I miss trying to figure out how to answer your philosophical questions, because as I strengthened your faith, I also strengthened mine.

I miss the mom/provider I was when I bought you school supplies and groceries and clothes and just unnecessary indulgences. I miss laughing with you as we went about our errands.

I even miss the mom/referee I was when sibling rivalry raised its ugly head.

But mostly, I miss the mom/friend I was as you grew into adolescence. We were all just becoming such good friends and establishing an adult relationship.

I will also miss the mom I will never be to you as you

would have grown older. I will miss the worrying mother I will not be as you would have begun to date and drive. I will miss the rejoicing mother I will not be as you graduate, get married, and have a life of your own.

I will miss being the grandmother to your children I will not be. I will miss the full circle I will not see as you, my children, would have had children of your own.

And last, selfishly, I will miss the love and support I will not have from you when I am old and feeble.

I miss you and I miss the me I was when I was with you, but I must say good-bye to motherhood.

I was passionate for God. I really enjoyed going to church and worshipping Him. I enjoyed living, but when my children died, the passion for living just left. I was not motivated to do anything and all I wanted was to have them back.

Maybe that's the depression part of grief work. Whatever it is, it was a difficult emotion for me, just being without purpose. I was "existing" but I was not "becoming" which is what Existential Therapy was supposed to do for me. I didn't really care about anything or becoming anyone.

There was enough inborn work ethic in me that I automatically went to work every day. I had a need to pay my own way and I didn't want charity but other than some low-level motivation like that, I was just existing. I was a widow and childless mother. I was reduced to nothing. It was left to me to build my new identity.

For a while I ate food out of a can — when I ate.

Sometimes I didn't eat because it just didn't matter. That is a bad feeling.

Initially the things that must be taken care of brought on by a death in the family kept me very busy. When I tried to get back to some organization in my life, I experienced "busyness". I had an urgency to take care of things which was partly due to a need to avoid thinking.

The Physical Pain

The physical pain that I experienced after the death of my family was very real, too. I felt like someone had beaten me over the head with a baseball bat and left me to walk around dazed and confused.

My heart physically ached and at times I had a numbness in my chest. I know now there is a true heartache and it's not just a cliché used in songs. It was a discomfort that I could not escape. I tried walking, going to different places, getting involved in different things, but nothing relieved the pain. It would stop for a little while. I would fall asleep but when I would wake up, it would still be there and I would cry for indefinite periods of time.

There was also a mental numbness like a paralysis and I felt I could not think or see straight. All of my physical senses were dull. Maybe that was a lingering effect from the disorientation of being in shock.

The first few days after the funeral I had a lot of personal decisions to make. There was no one but me, like a lone survivor in a plane crash on a desert island. I felt so alone and cut off from everything I knew and loved.

I bitterly resented being a widow and having to clean up David's mess. He and I had made no preparations for me to handle something like this. I would have welcomed a stable person to have taken me under his or her wing and provided the wisdom needed to make these decisions that had to be made. But in reality, which is what all widows must face, there was no one there to help make these important decisions. I had to decide for myself what I was going to do with the rest of my life.

Loss Was A Long List

When my therapist asked me to list all of the things I felt that I had lost, it didn't seem like such a monumental task, but I confess now, I never could have dreamed of all the things I lost. I lost my way of life, my children, my husband, my house, my job, my furniture, and my identity. But what is so hard to face is that I lost everything from my past life — it's all gone and there's not one "cotton-picking" thing I can do about it. It is so *unfair*. But my therapist has convinced me that I still have me and I'll become whatever is possible to honor Amy and Eric. I have the memories of all the things I did right for them and what we did together can never die.

To come up with a simple illustration of how widespread my loss was, just think about a house exploding and incinerating everything — family, possessions — and you barely escape with your life. That's as close as I can come to explaining my plight.

You could probably explain a fire but you can't explain a father killing his children and himself. Also, a house can be rebuilt but you can't rebuild a dead family. If I could have ten other children, none of them could replace Eric and Amy.

I Lost The House

First I had a house in which I knew I couldn't live. I didn't go back home for five or six weeks. My home was my family and I could not bear the thoughts of ever living there again without them.

I was not mentally able to work so I was forced to give up my job, too — not because they didn't want me back but because I couldn't function well enough to be responsible for other people's lives. A Med Tech has to be well-trained and alert.

I was so angry with David that in one of my irrational moments I thought, "I'll go back and refurbish that house so that it will not remind me of anything in the past. I'll live there and continue on with my life like it never happened." When reality set in, I knew I could never live there again without the ones who used to animate it. Even the puppy was gone and no one was there to give it life.

How could I walk into that kitchen without seeing my little Amy on the floor? I couldn't walk those stairs without seeing David sitting there with the blood all over him and the walls, or look out of that window where the blood stains had been so visible that the news people had taken a picture of it from the outside. I could never have looked passed the image of Eric lying there on the bedroom floor, face down in his own blood, spilled at the hands of his father.

I couldn't go back home nor could I go back to my job but where would I go and where would I work? I'm thankful that I had David's brother and his wife who let me stay with them temporarily and then later, I stayed with some friends in Montgomery.

I Lost My Stability

I recall seeing the movie, "Forrest Gump," and thinking how stupid it was for him to run across the United States. Then after my family died, I could really relate to Forrest and his need to run and punish his body to take the pressure off his mind. I could not stay in one place very long. I just wanted to keep going and avoid having to think. I would get very restless if I stayed in one place more than two or three days. I'd have a compulsion to put everything in the car and go somewhere else, but this was a pain from which I couldn't run away.

I had all of this energy, pent up anger, pent up grief and I could do nothing with it and wanted a sublimation such as walking to get rid of it. I wanted to walk to California. I don't know why I didn't. The avoidance became so strong that I was convinced that if I could walk hard enough, or drive far enough, I wouldn't have to face my fears and pain.

The "dis-ease" was always with me. Everywhere I went, I would be reminded of my children. The supermarket or Wal-Mart reminded me of them because they loved going there. Every section of the store held some significance to one or other of the children from the time they were little until they died. So, Wal-Mart became a very sad place for me to go. Eric thought going to the grocery store was kinda neat and he always wanted to go with me, so for a while going to the grocery store was a sad experience for me. There are many other places where we went together as a family that became sad places. Almost anywhere I went I was reminded of David, Eric, Amy, or sometimes all three. I've had to learn to cope with those constant reminders of my family now that I am a widow and childless mother.

At times I wanted to run away to some place where I would not be reminded of the past, but some reminders brought back good memories, too. Even though I am sad that they aren't with me, I cherish these good memories. So, it's been a mixed bag. For a while my emotions were up and down, but now as the healing has begun in earnest, things are beginning to settle down and I am regaining my stability.

I Lost My Furniture

In addition to my house and job, I also had to get rid of my furniture. I had to pack up all of the things that meant so much to David, my children and me. The thought of putting them in storage or selling them at a garage sale was so painful. Little things like baseball cards, trophies, bulletin boards, notes from school, school books, tapes, record players, roller blades, bicycles, clothes, pretty dresses, play clothes, tennis shoes, bathing suits, toothbrushes — that were such a vital part of my

162

children had to go somewhere. Though I didn't want to, I had to clean the house out and do something with everything in it.

What about our bedroom suite with the bed in which David and I had slept for so long? We had picked it out together and it was one of the nicer pieces of furniture we had in our house. How could I sleep in that same bed without being reminded of the man who had fathered my children and then killed them? It might seem strange but I didn't want any part of it. The living room reminded me of a family that no longer existed and made me tremendously depressed. I could not come in from work and look at the furniture that was a part of my life that is now history.

So I put everything that David and I had worked so hard for on the auction block and I took a tremendous financial loss on it. The sentimental things that I could keep I boxed up and put in storage.

For a while I would pull out some pieces of their clothes and just cry over them. Eric's tee shirts seemed to hold a special meaning so I kept some of them and I wear them occasionally to remember him. I kept some of Amy's tee shirts, too, and some of her other clothes and I wear them sometimes to remind me of her. Some of their personal belongings were so difficult for me to look at that I was compelled to give them away.

I Lost My Identity

The main task of therapy for me is to re-establish my identity. Imagine having amnesia and getting lost in an unfamiliar world, not knowing who you are. For so many years I had been a wife and a mother. It all seemed so natural and I guess I had taken it all for granted. Motherhood was the most enjoyable thing I had ever experienced and suddenly, like vanishing ink, all the mothering and wife things were gone.

It was the most sickening feeling. I experienced death every day but I couldn't die. I often wonder if I've died and gone to Hell. Is this my bottomless pit, my fire that burns and never goes out? Are the worms gnawing at my stomach? My therapist says the difference in this Hell and the Devil's Hell is that I can eventually get out of the one I'm in now and I think I am getting out.

I went from being young to being old in one day. I had been married but I wasn't divorced. I was a widow and widows are supposed to be old. I didn't fit the single parent scene because, even though I was a mother I didn't have any children. When I tried to describe myself, it kept coming out. I'm a wife with no husband and a mother with no children. Should I start over? I was totally single — not partly single — and I had a love/hate relationship with my new identity. I loved being free but I wasn't willing to pay the price of freedom — trade my husband and children for freedom — no way!

What does the word single mean? What was right for me to want for my life? Was I suppose to want a family again? Was I suppose to decide to be single for a while and throw myself into my career? And, to tell the truth, none of those choices appealed to me because all I wanted was a family and career, but family superseded career.

I went to a function for singles and felt so out of place. When I looked at all those people, I said, "I don't fit in here." I would go to the Sunday School class that had been so meaningful in the past and I didn't fit there anymore. I wasn't married but I didn't feel single. Maybe we need a "misfit" class at church. I couldn't compare my children with my friends' children so I didn't fit in with mothers anymore. If I had never experienced what I've experienced, I could never have known the disappointments that pop up every day, many times a day. I was just a puzzle piece that didn't belong to any puzzle.

Well, I was still alive, terminally ill and a member of society, so I had to fit somewhere — but where? I had to make myself fit because I couldn't be so intimidated by this new world that I couldn't live my life. I had no choice. It was either swim or drown. During my struggle I might have gone under a couple of times but I refused to sink for the final count. All I had to do was stop fighting and let depression devour me. It was my call. I chose to swim and things began to improve.

While trying to cope with this single lifestyle, I did some things right but I did some things wrong, too. Since my therapist and I want this book to help others in their struggles, I'm going to mention some things I did right. Remember that I had no blueprint for this building process. I have found no precedent — no pattern left by anyone who had the exact kind of circumstances in which I found myself. So I paved my own road while coping with grief. I would have to live with the consequences of my choices. In my vulnerable condition I could easily have followed everyone's advice and been thoroughly confused but I chose to do it my way.

My New Home

Eventually I was able to get an apartment in Montgomery and have a place that was more like home. I went back to my old job which I had given up to move with David to Virginia. It was the same shift and schedule that I had had before. Most of the work was very familiar to me so it wasn't mentally taxing. Work was a refuge to which I could go. The people with whom I worked were very kind, said many helpful things and wanted to help me get back on my feet.

What I Did Right

One of the things I did right was to spend some money on myself. Dr. Gunnells told me to buy whatever I had always wanted but couldn't afford, as long as it was reasonable. So I bought myself some clothes. I followed the advice of my friends and tried to improve my physical appearance. During my marriage to David, like many women I know, I had ignored my physical appearance to a great degree and had resigned myself to be a grumpy, middle-aged woman. My self-image was bringing me down so I spent some money on clothes and make-up, lost some weight, changed my hair style, and all of these things cheered me up a little bit.

Dr. Gunnells told me that when one feels like he or she needs to take control over his or her life, it often begins with changing the way we look. It's temporary when one is in grief but it helps.

I began to make myself more attractive in case someone came along that I might want to date. Oh yes, the word, date — that's a scary word to someone who's been out of the dating business for so long. I didn't know how to start dating.

Another thing I did right was to take the advice of one of my friends and go to counseling. I was resistant at first because I really didn't want to grieve. I liked being in denial. I still wanted to sweep the whole thing under the carpet and pretend like it didn't happen. I could only take it in increments. I couldn't take it all at one time. Thankfully, my therapist insisted that I keep my power and control the pace of the therapy and grieve at my own tempo. I don't know what I would have done without therapeutic support.

I determined to move on to a positive level from the very moment I discovered the bodies of my family. Right then, I decided that I had to find a way to overcome this total injustice. I was not going to let it ruin my life. I had a strong suspicion that David, however twisted his thinking was, did this as a way to hurt me one last time. His passive/aggressive disorder had turned aggressive toward me without ever putting his hands on me. It is my nature to be stubborn and I was not going to bend nor break, run nor hide. I decided to take my anger out on him by overcoming what seemed like total defeat. I vowed and declared that David would not win in this situation. He would not bring me down in defeat.

Determination and anger were driving forces to win whatever battles were left for me to fight. It is hard to fight an enemy you can't see. "Reality" was the enemy.

One of the most difficult results of being single again was coming home all excited about what had happened during the day and no one being there to ask me how my day had gone. It didn't matter.

My house was neat as a pin but I yearned to see roller blades, dirty clothes and rings in the bathtub. It was terrible to be alone.

My Need For Companionship

I was desperate for companionship. I was not just lonely every now and then. I was lonely every day — every wakened minute. Every day when I came in from work, the house was quiet as a tomb. I had been used to being met at the door by David or one of the children, or sometimes all of them. I felt loved and needed and now — zilch — nothing. All the joking and teasing, the clowning, and most of all, the planning we did together was gone. The only living thing I could talk to was my cat and she wouldn't talk back. This set-up was very, very heartrending for me.

A lot of my friends cautioned me about getting married so quickly and I appreciated their concern. To those who wish to judge widows or widowers who marry soon after the death of a spouse, I can only say, if you haven't been there, you are not the expert. Just walk in our shoes one day and you'll see what it's like. Going from a house teeming with life to a cold, quiet, spiritless set of walls is next to Hell, if it's not Hell. I could have been abducted and chopped up into little pieces and no one would have known because I was not accountable to anyone. Such a thought was very unsettling and insecure.

I had no one to affirm me. Even though David was so caught up in his world of pain and pain killers, at least he was there and in an immature way showed some compassion toward me. No one was there now to contradict me or discipline me by making me rethink what I was doing or thinking.

This "aloneness" was causing me to become selfish and cynical and I didn't like what I saw because I have always despised selfishness. I had taught my children to respect themselves but they didn't have a selfish bone in them. They had pride but not arrogance. Becoming selfish was contrary to what I wanted my children to be and it hurt me to feel that way myself.

Another thing about being single and devoid of companionship was the tremendous sexual pressure that I felt. I think this was partly because I had lost my identity and had let myself go physically. I had begun to feel crummy and considered myself unattractive.

I longed for some kind of affirmation from a man. I needed to be connected and enjoy real companionship and so the sexual pressure was so great and began testing my self-discipline.

Along with the sexual pressure, I also felt a need to rebel. I kept thinking, "Okay, God, I've done things your way for so long and now look what I got, so I'm going to do things my way and see what happens." I even entertained having a baby out of wedlock, something that I would have never considered or dreamed of before. I thought, "Why not? I could get pregnant, send the man on his way and I won't have to fool with him but I can have what I want — a baby!" This makes me wonder if David had not begun to feel that the children were what I wanted and I didn't need him anymore.

Fortunately, I had some friends who loved me enough to bear with me through all of my foolish thinking. I am truly grateful for friends because without them I doubt if I would have made it through those early months when I was so angry and rebellious.

Finally I started dating and that almost became an obsession to me. I thought, "I've stuck with one man for 18 years and look what happened. There's no way that I can stick with one man again." I wanted to date a lot of different people and I did date some until I met the man to whom I am now married. Some of the men I dated were not good for me and I knew they would be detrimental to my future. I didn't want to head down a path from which there was no return. I decided to date only men that I would want to marry and that would improve me as a person. Not to overstate this but the sexual pressure was so strong, I needed someone who could be a potential mate for me. The scripture that says it's better to marry than to burn (desire sex) became meaningful to me. I saw before me two paths: (1) a path of being single without self-control, or (2) of getting married and practicing the discipline a person of my moral thinking should. I wanted my life in control. My prayers were for God to send me the right person and I think the way I met my present husband, God answered my prayers.

We fell in love very quickly and we both wanted and needed each other. We decided to get married and we have a very good relationship. He is my support and he's been there to help me through the intense grief so many times.

No one likes to be alone when sick and helpless. It was a scary time for me. Some people are not cut out to live alone. I needed someone with whom to eat my meals and with whom to watch TV. I guess if one wanted to they could take care of the sexual needs outside of marriage but the loneliness is more than sex, it's security and friendship.

I never wanted to be single. David chose that for me. He could have avoided making me a widow and childless mother but he didn't. I hated being single and I resented David for what he did to me. I hated the cards that I had been dealt. They stunk! But I had to play the hand I had been dealt because I refused to lose the game.

Do My Needs Count?

I needed a husband to meet my needs, both physically and emotionally. My sexuality was the only part of me that my children didn't share. It's like everything else reminded me of them but I needed the healing power of loving, married sex to be a "Balm in Gilead" for me. Sex as God intended it is pure and healing and a child of God deserves this kind of love.

My new husband and I both healed together. He is

divorced but unlike me he still has his two children. David not only abandoned me but he took my two children from me.

While some parts of me were dying, the person in me began to come alive in the relationship I have with Charles, my new love. I can be a mom to his two boys but I don't have to be their primary mother figure. Dr. Gunnells helped me to avoid trying to be "super mom". Our relationship will grow but I will never try to take the place of their real mom. I understand motherhood because I learned so much from Eric and Amy. I affirm Charles' two sons and they affirm me when they say such things as, "Kim, I'm glad you are with my dad", or "Kim, I love you". I need their hugs and kisses and I need to mother them on a limited basis.

I can finish my grief work and also have compassion for Charles at the same time. My therapist says that family oriented people marry much more quickly than those who didn't like family life.

I have stepped out of the looking glass of Alice in Wonderland from one life to another and I can only make the best of the one I've got now. I am still a childless mother as far as Eric and Amy are concerned. They'll never be replaced even if I choose to have another child myself.

Here I am — coping with my past, present and future all at the same time. I am carving my path the best way I know how. I'm learning every day. As my therapist says, "I'm a lifelong learner" like everyone else who tries to make the best out of life.

I'm a survivor. I must do it my way. I've never attempted

suicide but if I hadn't had my husband, I might not have gotten through the pain. I think I did the right thing by getting married. I am convinced that my needs count. I am a worthwhile person. I need to be needed, wanted, useful, loved and appreciated to be a whole person. The only place I ever found that kind of relationship was in my family. I need a family to be complete or at least to practice being complete.

Reality Therapy has taught me to be realistic, responsible, and right. If I pursue this course as best I can, the *unfairness* of my plight will ease but I doubt it will ever go away. It's still *the most unfair thing I've ever heard.*

Friendly Advice

One of the first things young couples need to do is determine what to do in the event of the early death of one or other of the spouses. I was forced to make arrangements that I never dreamed I would have to deal with so early.

Every family should have a will, adequate life insurance, burial plots, and have some idea where their home base is. We kinda knew our life had settled in the Montgomery area so that's where I returned to get my feet on the ground.

A widow should not tell anyone but the necessary people about life insurance settlements or other large sums of money. She should find someone trustworthy to advise her in any business deals in which she might become involved. It is advisable not to make hasty decisions of any major proportion for at least six months to one year otherwise she might act on her emotions rather than her reason. Many widows give large sums of money to organizations to honor their husbands only to find out later that they have created a financial hardship for themselves.

When everything is planned, it cuts down on the margin of error the grieving widow might make.

David and I had obviously not planned for what happened to my family but I hope my experience will help others to be prepared for the unexpected. I would like to use my "on-the-job training" to help those who are faced with widowhood, suicide or mental illness.

It really helps to have a good church, good family and good friends when life tumbles in.

Conclusion

The story you have just read is true. After I had completed the rough draft, Kim brought me pictures of her children and it really became real to me. I have left out names of people and institutions, but the names of Kim's children and husband are their real names because she wanted them to be memorialized in this book.

Now that it has been over a year since her children died, it's yesterday's news to us but it's not to her. It's fresh on her mind every day and she wants to talk about Amy and Eric. To most people, it's old hat, a tired subject. Even Kim's family seldom mention their names. When she is crying or sad, most of her friends and co-workers change the subject. She says, "How I wish someone would ask me to see their pictures, things they drew or made, what their rooms were like, or what they laughed about."

You see, all she has left to talk about is their past. She has no present or future with them, but they are still a part of her every moment and she wishes desperately people would be interested in hearing her talk about them. But, it's yesterday's news.

I asked Kim to tell us more about herself and her family.

More About Eric

I remember when I began to learn about "the birds and the bees" and how babies came from their mother's tummy that I looked down at my stomach and thought, "One day I'll have a baby in there." I guess all little girls dream of having their own children and I was no different.

I was so excited when I became pregnant with Eric and I thought all my dreams were coming together. I remember the flutter of life as I felt him move for the first time, talking and singing to him while he was still in the womb, and when he was born thinking how awesome it was that life could come from my body and a son at that. He was beautiful, mine, and that was all that counted.

Eric was a comical toddler. We thought he looked like "Tweety Bird" with those big brown eyes, round pink cheeks and small chin. He would take his clothes off, put them in the toilet, and say, "Wash, wash".

He loved Superman and sports and once when looking at

his room, I told him, "Eric, you seem to value strength because all these things in your room have that theme", and he agreed. Even the name Eric means "strong leader" and that's what I was grooming him to be.

As Eric grew, he continued to excel in academics. He was chosen for magnet programs and won an award for poetry in the sixth grade. Eric was very responsible and I could always depend on him to do whatever I asked him to do.

As he became older he seemed to become quieter and more shy and I sensed that he was having problems with his self-confidence; however, to me he was perfect and I continued to tell him how talented and handsome he was. But his teenage years found a way to rip out his self-confidence.

He was very insightful and developed an interest in spiritual things at an early age. Eric was always asking about God and even asked me, "Mom, draw God." I think Eric was having problems juggling peer pressure and being a Christian. He wanted to be accepted as being "cool" and this caused him to hesitate to get involved in church as Amy did.

Ironically, the night before he died, Eric and I were discussing James Dobson's book, *Life on the Edge* which I had assigned him to read for the summer. He said, "Mom, this is a great book. Even if you hadn't asked me to read it, I would have wanted to because it will really help me." We talked about heaven and who would probably be there waiting for us and how important it is for us to "be there" when we die.

How were we to know that in less than twenty-four hours

he would "be there". I take comfort in the fact that he is with Jesus, without fear or pain, and will meet me at the "east gate".

Eric was gaining self-confidence and received an academic achievement award for that school year. He was developing into a man and I was proud to see him doing so well.

However, tension was brewing between David and Eric. They didn't seem to be able to agree on anything. On one occasion when Eric was crying in his room, I went in where he was and he asked me, "Mom, why does daddy hate me so much?" I reassured him that his dad did not hate him but that he was just being irritable. Deep inside, however, I wondered the same thing.

More About Amy

When Eric was a toddler, I became pregnant with Amy. She was planned and I prayed for a girl but I would have loved a boy just as much.

When Amy was born she was smaller than Eric and she became the real baby doll that I had dreamed of as a child. We named her Amy which means "beloved". I remember how complete I felt when we brought her home from the hospital.

Amy was calmer and more content than Eric had been. She was sweet and cuddly and loved being held and touched. She was my "little china doll", and since she was so tiny, we caused her to talk baby talk a little too long.

In kindergarten her teachers said she was immature but as she grew older, it became apparent that she had a developmental problem. Amy had a hard time in school. Tests revealed that

178

she had both Attention Deficit Disorder and another learning disability. Both of us had to work hard to keep her on her appropriate grade level. Even though she went to tutors, took medication, and attended special classes, school work never came easy. But she survived because she was very social and seemed to make friends easily. I tried very hard to keep her confidence up when it was "nailed to the ground" by her failures. My maternal instinct made me want to fight all her battles and protect her from disappointment. She would cry and say, "I'm just too dumb." It was hard to find the balance with Amy as when to push and when to leave her alone.

She told me once, "Mom, I'm just not 'purfect'. You expect me to be 'purfect' and I'm just not 'purfect'." Amy taught me that none of us are 'purfect'. She demanded unconditional love. I had loved Eric for doing well and I learned from Amy that love is not earned, and I learned to love her whether she passed another grade or not. Now she's finished her course, graduated to another life and is studying under the Master Teacher.

Amy was very kindhearted and thoughtful and even won a "Random Act of Kindness" award for helping someone at school pick up some papers they had dropped. When I came home from work tired, she would fix snacks and coffee and bring them to me. She loved to cook and I enjoyed helping her plan meals and cooking them for her dad.

Amy loved her dad so much. I wonder how he could have shot her three times. How could he have wanted to hurt his little "beloved"? The only answer lies in the fact that he was mentally unbalanced at the time. He didn't know what he was doing.

Amy was really beginning to blossom in her thirteenth year. She had joined the youth group at church, was baptized, and had begun to talk to people about Christ. Two weeks later she would see Christ in person.

The mental picture I have of Amy's little face when I saw her that day will always be with me. It was gray with a tinge of orange. She had a peaceful look yet I knew it was a look of death. My emotional mind still hasn't caught up with it. Sometimes I just think, "Where is she? She'll be back soon."

The other day I was going shopping and for a brief moment I thought, "I need to see if Amy wants to go." It's just a strange feeling to know that she's dead and yet not really accept it at the same time, even though it has been a year.

Amy had just gotten old enough to be able to enjoy things with me and perhaps when she got older, she would have had new interests and I would not have been included. I will never know. I lost my mother at the age of ten and my daughter at the age of thirteen. Maybe it was never meant for me to experience a full and complete mother-daughter relationship.

More About David

I don't know if I will ever miss David or grieve for him like I do for the children. It bothers me because I feel like I should be grieving for him. My therapist says it will come sooner or later and that I might need special help when it begins.

I'm learning to forgive him. I'm trying. I'm angry with him but I also feel sorry for him because he was a desperate man. He didn't understand what was going on in his life and didn't know how to battle it.

How could I have known that David would become so irrational that he would take Eric's life? David had never been a violent man. I never dreamed he was capable of anything brutal like that. If I had only known, I would have taken the kids and left but I stayed because I thought they needed their father. It was the worst decision I could have made. Our home had become so chaotic especially when Eric provoked David or when David came home from work ranting and raving.

Please indulge me to rethink the incident on Friday night before the suicide/homicide on Monday. You might recall that when we were at the beach that David could not sleep, went to the car in his underwear, and seemed to search the car in every nook and corner. I now wonder if the pleasure of this family vacation was not the telling event that caused him to see a blissful resolution to his dilemma and made him want to end his suffering there in that beautiful place.

Could he have had the gun hidden in the car and struggled to decide whether this was the time to use it or not? Remember how bizarre I said his behavior was. Could he have been trying to find enough pain killers in all of the nineteen bottles he had in the car to end his life that night? In hindsight, I believe he was more disturbed than I had ever seen him. His every action, including his insistence for sex, seemed to have been a compulsion. It was so strange, so out of character for David, and he had never been so insensitive toward me before.

Again, I really wonder about that night and wish I knew what was on his mind. It's always a question but there's never an answer.

Some clues seem to indicate that David methodically calculated what he did. The gun was stored in one place and the bullets in another. David had conspicuously left the American Express card on the dresser so I could find it. He did not come to bed at all on Sunday night before that fatal Monday. When I think about that day, I wonder what went on in David's mind and what trauma my children had to endure in their own house.

More About Me

If I live a normal life span, it seems like such a long time before I will be able to be with my children. I miss them so much.

I feel like I am beginning to live again now that Charles has entered the picture. He gives me comfort when I am with him but I am tired of the struggle, of trying to live the Christian life, of trying to keep my equilibrium. Sometimes just existing is the hardest thing for me.

I have resolved to make the most out of my life. I don't want to get to the judgment and have Jesus say, "What did you do with the forty years I gave you after the kids died?" I don't want to have to say, "Well, nothing, I wasted it." I am not going to do that. I am going to do something to help people like me.

I can trudge onward, try to make some sense out of the rest of my life, try to be a good wife to my new husband, or I can grieve over the fact that I will never see my children again and not be able to do anything productive.

I hope my story will help others in their journey through life for when we hear of each other's struggles, we can clasp our hands across the distance and form a bond through the fellowship of suffering.

Perhaps you have never experienced this fellowship but trust me, if you live long enough you will. It will almost always take you by surprise and be an unwelcome guest. Pain by its very nature is something we all wish to avoid at all cost. Once you got into this book, you might have even hesitated to read the entire story because you were afraid of the pain that jumped from its pages. But, as you probably already know, God has given us beautiful defense mechanisms to keep our emotional pain from destroying us.

If you have gotten nothing else out of this book, perhaps you have seen God working patiently with me as I shook my fist at Him in the throws of my pain. I hope you have seen a glimpse of His marvelous grace as He allowed me to survive the devastating blows that I experienced. He was infinitely patient with me and not one bit intimidated by my foolish questions and doubts. You probably saw me question, challenge, rebel against Him and at times, demand answers and reasons for the tragic events that have transpired over my life span, and especially July 17, 1995.

I hope you could see on the pages that I have submitted

myself to Him and learned that He is sovereign, and that I now trust His higher ways. Though what has happened to me is so *unfair*, I believe it will all make sense someday.

May we all join together in the fellowship of healing after the pain is gone.

Closing the Book

Eric had started a daily journal about his life and his first entry was on July 12, five days before he died. As I read the entries in his journal, I saw a typical, yet somewhat advanced, fifteen year old.

His writing was so honest and uninhibited. He was excited about the family vacation to Hilton Head, South Carolina, which ended up being Myrtle Beach. On July 13 as the family was traveling, he wrote, "I write again as the car flows across ribbons of highway." This is indicative of his ability to express himself in writing.

He had written a letter to a girl asking her to be his girlfriend and he wrote in his journal that he was curious about her reactions and hoped she would accept him, but he had his doubts.

The long trip from Virginia to South Carolina became tiring and he wrote, "All this waiting for fleeting pleasure dulls me." There were signs that he was already becoming depressed like his mother and father.

Upon our return from vacation he wrote, "I'm kinda depressed since our trip ended but I think my spirits will lift when I talk to my girlfriend later."

On December 12, 1995, I felt compelled to write one last entry in Eric's journal and it reads as follows:

Dear Eric, My Son, My Son,

I hesitate to write in your journal because it was to have been your diary but you can no longer write on its pages and yet it is now a valuable part of your precious life, my son. Your life should have filled these pages and many other books but your story was cut short and I weep for you, my precious son.

As I close your diary, I must symbolically close the book on Amy's, David's, and your life. A book will last for eons but its story line must close at some point. Only God is eternal — everything else must end.

I wish all of you could have lived according to my expectations, but you died much too soon and without warning.

With the closing of this book that Dr. Gunnells and I have spent several months writing, I now must close the book on my life with you and let you rest and enjoy eternity while I enjoy your memory.

I am allowing this closure to take place because I must, not because I want to, and no matter how much time passes, what happened to my family will always be *the most unfair thing I've ever heard.*

Postscript

About the time this book was going to press, a casual acquaintance of Kim's committed suicide, and like a bolt of lightning, she began to reopen all of her wounds caused by the suicide of her mother and David. Like a woman possessed, she began to say, "We've got to do something about suicide. Something has to be done." During her next session, I recognized that Kim's anger for David was gone. She was accepting the fact that he was dead, never coming back, and her grief work for him had now begun in earnest. Now she knows she will never hold his hands again.

Kim feels bad for Charles, who has now become her new husband, that she has begun to revisit her pain but she is relieved to know that she is at least beginning to let it go. I now think she can totally forgive David. I am thankful that it is about over. Kim accepts the fact that David was sick and unable to know what he was doing, and she can pray, "Father, forgive him, for he knew not what he was doing."